Religious Liberty

AMENDMENT 1

Congress shall make no law respecting an establishment
of religion, or prohibiting the free exercise thereof;
or abridging the freedom of speech, or of the press;
or the right of the people peaceably to assemble,
and to petition the government for a redress of grievances.

Religious Liberty

The Christian Roots of
Our Fundamental Freedoms

E. GLENN HINSON

Glad River

Contents

Publisher's Foreword
to the Revised Edition

GLAD RIVER PUBLICATIONS is very pleased that its first book is Dr. Glenn Hinson's *Religious Liberty: The Christian Roots of Our Fundamental Freedoms* (first published in 1974 under the title *Soul Liberty*). No more timely book can be imagined than this, especially in this bicentennial of the Bill of Rights.

Virtually all Christian communions have come to see the central importance of religious liberty as a Christian doctrine. One group in particular — the Baptists — have a right to be proud of the role they played in seeing this doctrine embodied in our Constitution. But as Reuben Herring wrote in the foreword to the first edition, "Tragically, Baptists in America are almost totally unaware of perhaps their greatest contribution to the free world" — the doctrine of religious liberty. Whether all Baptists in America are unaware of this contribution, it is true these days that Baptists in the South seem ready to renounce it. It is also true that recent Supreme Court decisions indicate that our nation as a nation is retreating from its original commitment to personal liberty.

One reason, therefore, for publishing a revised edition of this book is to remind Baptists of their good heritage. But it also serves to call other Christian churches to step into the breach, as it were, deserted by Baptists in the South, and take up the defense of this belief.

There is a second reason Glad River is pleased to publish this book. The movement in the world at large (if not in America) is toward freedom. This movement is seen above all in the recent events

7

in Eastern Europe, and also in the development of base communities (roughly equivalent to what Baptists call "the local church") in countries of the so-called third world. In these areas, people are demanding the fundamental freedoms we in this country already enjoy. Perhaps this new edition of Dr. Hinson's book will find its way to these people and confirm them in their struggle to be free.

It has been a joy working with Dr. Hinson on this book. All fledgling publishers should be as lucky as I have been to have as their first author a person of such scholarship, integrity, and Christian grace.

— BILL THOMASON, Publisher
July 1991

Preface to the Revised Edition

In 1991 Americans celebrate the two hundredth anniversary of the ratification of the Bill of Rights, the first ten amendments to the U.S. Constitution. Article 1, especially, "Congress shall make no law respecting an establishment of religion, or prohibiting the free exercise thereof, . . . " holds significance for all religious groups in America, Protestant and Catholic, but especially for Baptists, for they contributed more than any other religious group to its inclusion in the Constitution.

Curiously, on the two hundredth anniversary many Baptists in the United States have forgotten why their forebears fought so fiercely for religious freedom as the most basic of all freedoms. Few know any longer the names of Smyth and Helwys and Bunyan in England or Williams and Backus and Leland in America. Sadder still, few can comprehend such radical commitments as these made that they would give their very lives to assure freedom for the Word of God.

Why have Baptists forgotten? Many reasons can be cited, I am sure, but none would be more significant than the shift in the situation of Baptists in America from minority to majority consciousness. Oppressed and persecuted people cry out for freedom, in this case freedom to follow the dictates of conscience in matters of religion. The majority cannot understand such pleas. "Why don't they accept the truth safeguarded by the established church? Why must they have freedom that may well lead them into heresy? We must protect them from erroneous consciences. The welfare of our society depends on right doctrine and worship."

Only in the United States has Baptist consciousness changed on this matter, for only in America have Baptists attained anything like majority status. East of Texas and South of the Mason-Dixon line, Baptists have what Martin E. Marty calls an "Empire." Migration to the Sun Belt may well erode this position, but, as things now stand, Southern Baptists represent from 25 to 100 percent of the population in virtually every county. They have had the South on a roll in the last half century, and, for their success, they are paying a high price in loss of identity as Baptists. Now other minority groups — Episcopalians, Presbyterians, Methodists, and even Roman Catholics — hold up the torch of liberty many Baptists have thrown aside.

This book was written in 1974 with ardent hope that Baptists in the South might rediscover the doctrine they were rapidly letting slip away. What has happened in the Southern Baptist Convention since, however, makes recovery of such thinking on the part of Southern Baptists as a whole appear bleak. Within this convention, nevertheless, one will find those who have not forgotten and who still want to lift up their voices with those of their forebears on behalf of religious liberty. I have made this revision with them in mind.

I am grateful to the Baptist General Association of Virginia, especially the Rev. D. Gwynn Davis, Jr., Director of Christian Life Concerns, for initiating this revision.

Chapter 1

What Is Religious Liberty?

THIS STUDY concerns a doctrine that Baptists have cherished above all others from the beginning of their history. The term "soul liberty," which the earliest Baptists used, may perplex a modern reader. The word "soul" is used often today — "soul food," "soul sleep," "soul music," "soul brother." Usually it designates depth of identity in black culture. The idea of deep feeling would not have been alien to the understanding of soul liberty among seventeenth-century English groups, such as Baptists and Quakers, with whom it originated. They sought true liberty. For them, this meant *religious* liberty! They had in mind the liberty to follow the dictates of the Spirit and the Scriptures in forming churches, and the liberty to worship according to the dictates of conscience rather than "human" prescription.

Why a Historical Study?

This will be a doctrinal study from a strongly historical perspective. Why historical? Why not simply biblical?

The first answer to these questions is that, in this instance, we have a doctrine that has biblical grounds but that Christians grasped slowly. The Scriptures, even of the New Testament, do not lay down clear, explicit statements about religious liberty. Under the Old Covenant, Israel lived under a theocracy that wedded religion and civil affairs. The issue of religious liberty never occurred to them. Each obeyed the covenant with God or quietly suffered penalties for violating it. In the New Testament era, the early Christians lived under the totalitarian regime of Rome. They did not have a heritage of religious liberty. They represented a tiny minority. They sought to discharge a mission, not to mount a forceful campaign for religious freedom.

It was the pursuit of their mission, the proclamation of the gospel to all, that made these first Christians conscious of the need for religious liberty. For Christians the issue has always been the freedom to witness to the good news of Jesus Christ to win adherents. Other religions have not comprehended this. For other world religions today — Buddhism, Hinduism, Islam — the issue usually has been to *conserve* the adherents they already have.

Christianity is a strongly missionary faith. It must have freedom to discharge its mission. In the Roman Empire, which was usually tolerant, this soon posed a problem. First, it posed a problem with the Jews, who wanted Gentiles to become Jews before they became Christians. Later, it posed a problem with the Romans. The Romans tolerated Jews worshipping their ancestral God. But they could not understand why Romans would desert their ancestral gods to become Christians. Christianity, therefore, became an illegal religion, and Christians felt the lash of intolerance.

Roman intolerance reared its head in the New Testament era. There were spasmodic and scattered persecutions — under Nero (54–68 C.E.) and Domitian (81–96 C.E.). But these did not yet prompt the writing of impassioned or reasoned defenses of religious liberty. The first of these appeared in the next century. The New Testament has supplied Christians a seedbed for this doctrine in its fundamental Christian concepts. Later generations, faced with intolerance and persecution, planted, watered, and cultivated as the doctrine grew to a mature plant in the American religious experiment.

A second reason for treating the doctrine historically is that history will cast much light on its true character and on the difficulties in understanding and implementing it. The Christian contribution to the doctrine and the practice of religious liberty has been mixed. Brilliant and noble minds have both defended and denied religious freedom. They have quoted some of the same texts of Scripture in doing so. They have argued sometimes from the same fundamental principles. Augustine, and hundreds in imitation of him, argued that love demanded the use of coercion to cause heretics to join the Catholic Church. Others have argued with equal insistence that love, like God's love, could never coerce.

A third reason for using the historical approach is that it will offer some insights into current problems and dangers regarding religious liberty. The preservation of religious liberty requires constant and unfailing vigilance. It was obtained at a high price, and it is maintained at a high price. Some lessons from history reinforce our motive to conserve it.

What Is Religious Liberty?

Before we examine the doctrine of liberty in depth, it will be helpful to define it more closely. As I will use the term in this book, "religious liberty" means *the freedom of every human being, whether as an individual or in a group, from social coercion in religious matters*. It is not to be equated with freedom of choice or will or freedom of conscience. It includes these, but it is broader. Both of these have to do with interior matters over which society can exercise no control. In the Commonwealth era in England, for example, Oliver Cromwell could honestly avow that he would "meddle with no man's conscience" while refusing Roman Catholics the right to celebrate the Mass anywhere in the realm. Further, religious liberty is not the same as religious toleration. Tolerant persons may permit others to exercise their faith, but they do not recognize this as an inherent right. Governmentally, toleration is a policy of permitting forms of religious belief and worship not officially favored, established, or approved.

Religious liberty defined in this manner encompasses several freedoms. One is freedom of conscience, the right freely to determine what faith or creed one will follow. Others are freedom of religious expression, freedom of association, and freedom for corporate and institutional activities.

"Freedom of conscience" is an absolute, pure freedom. It concerns religion in its essence. God alone can exercise authority over the conscience. The state may inform the conscience of its citizens and limit immoral or injurious behavior, but it cannot presume to know what their consciences hold with respect to religion. It must grant liberty even to erroneous consciences.

The other three are qualified religious freedoms. They concern not only religious but fundamental human rights. They bear on rights that a state or a society does guarantee. Religious liberty in these spheres means freedom to speak or act in accordance with one's religious insights and values, so long as these do not injure someone else. A state should assure almost absolute freedom to communicate and associate. But there may be occasions when someone, from religious pretenses, would defame or slander another.

Freedom for corporate and institutional activities occasionally poses serious questions. Should a state, for instance, allow snake handling in religious cults when participants may undergo physical harm? Should a state coerce Jehovah's Witness parents to permit a blood transfusion for their child when they object on religious grounds? Should a state force conservative Amish to send their children to public schools in the interest of preparing them culturally to fit into society?

The nearly universal concern for religious liberty today encourages one to ask whether this is really a Christian doctrine. Does it originate in Christian insights, or is it merely a general human concern?

In response to this question, it should be admitted that the Christian concern for religious liberty applies to every human being, that we are not concerned for Christian liberty alone. In a study prepared for the World Council of Churches, Carrillo de Albornoz concluded that religious liberty was basic to all human rights on the following grounds: (1) It is itself a fundamental human right, not only individual but also social. (2) It is a human right that is distinctive from all others. (3) It is interrelated with all other human rights, for all other social rights derive from God's rule over human beings. (4) It is the foundation and guardian of all human rights in that respect for the highest loyalties of humankind will guarantee respect for lesser ones.[1]

On the other hand, religious liberty is a thoroughly Christian concept. There is a difference between the Christian understanding of the doctrine and its understanding by non-Christians. Other major religions confuse tolerance with religious freedom. They consider Christians intolerant because they cannot accept a hodgepodge mixture of Christianity with other religions. Christians consider them intolerant because they oppose the freedom of their adherents to leave their national religion for what they call a foreign one.

Secular humanists also approach the issue of religious liberty from another perspective. They are concerned that the civil society guarantee freedom for all persons in religion as in other basic rights. In a society composed of many religious views, the state has to prevent bitter quarrels without respect to any religious conviction. Thus church and state have to be entirely separate. The Christian understanding of religious liberty agrees with this (1) in its concern for social peace and harmony as one of society's tasks, (2) in the idea that a society may arbitrate disputes, and (3) in the concession that religious liberty includes the right to have no religion. It differs, however, in several ways. For the Christian: (1) Freedom is not based on natural human dignity but on God's gift; (2) it does not arise out of differences in religious views but out of inner freedom; (3) it is the state's role not merely to arbitrate disputes but to recognize fundamentally human rights.

Modern states represent a variety of attitudes toward religious liberty. (1) Totalitarian states deny it, for they require all human activities to submit to the authority of the state. (2) Secular democratic states are either indifferent or hostile to religion. (3) "Covenant" nations, in which church and state are allied, possibly endanger the freedom. (4) States that accept a specific confession endanger religious liberty in different ways. They may confuse the civil welfare with religious welfare (for example, Spain). The state may dictate the establishment of religion. In countries where non-Christian faiths control, freedom may be severely restricted.

Some Approaches to the Doctrine

In a fine study, *Protestant Faith and Religious Liberty*, Philip Wogaman has sorted out five approaches to the doctrine of religious liberty and added a sixth.[2] A review of these may help to clarify our method for defining the doctrine today. Three of these use essentially humanistic principles. Three are essentially Christian.

Humanistically Based Approaches

One approach, employed by Protestants and Other Americans United for the Separation of Church and State (POAU), argues from *the American tradition and constitutional authority for the separation of church and state*. Such an approach may be valuable from a legal standpoint, but it has weaknesses. Wogaman has criticized it on three grounds: (1) The tradition is complex and difficult to interpret in itself. (2) Vast changes in our social history increase the difficulty of interpretation. The founders of our country who drafted the Constitution did not visualize modern problems relating to government and church welfare, public school education, governmental research, global commitments to military and economic assistance paralleled by international church missionary and welfare activities, parochial school education, government regulation of the mass media, and more complicated forms of governmental taxation. (3) Religious liberty and separation of church and state are not necessarily twin principles.

Another approach, employed by Baptist church historian Winthrop Hudson and the distinguished Roman Catholic theologian John Courtney Murray, S.J., stresses the contribution of *pluralism*, the diversity of religious faiths, to religious liberty. More than anything else, it is argued, the diversity and conflict of religions have caused the institutionalization of religious liberty and nonestablishment of religion. The state has acted as an arbiter and peacemaker. American pluralism, moreover, has matured in America in ever greater diversity so as to assure religious liberty. Both the strength and the weakness of this approach are that it does not derive from religious faith. Nonbelievers can readily identify with it, but as Wogaman says, "A solution designed simply to preserve peace and harmony will, for the Christian, remain open to the possibility of negation by more ultimate norms."[3] Further, Wogaman asks, how much pluralism is required to guarantee religious liberty? A surer religious foundation would seem to be required.

A third approach, reflected in the two swords doctrine of the Middle Ages (spiritual and secular swords) and Luther's concept of orders of creation, bases religious liberty on the concept of *a limited state*. The state derives its power from God. It cannot have absolute power; that remains in God's hands. God also gives spiritual power, this time to the believers and the church. The difficulty with this view is that it does not give a rationale as to why a certain "right" ought to be institutionalized and guaranteed by the state.

Theologically Based Approaches

Because of these limitations in humanistically based approaches, many Christians have sought to develop alternatives based on more explicitly Christian grounds. The first of these approaches tries to correlate religious liberty with the Christian doctrine of human nature and response to God; that is, human *spiritual dignity and spiritual freedom*. Christian faith is meaningless, according to this view, if not entered into voluntarily. The essential nature of humankind requires freedom. Both the Christian view of grace and of redemption presupposes freedom. Only faith, and it free, puts one into relationship with God. The state cannot do so by coercion. This inner freedom bears on the social sphere, for human beings are social by nature. Since obedience must be voluntary, the best church government is that of the free church. The church cannot coerce.

A variation of this approach is Niels H. Soe's emphasis on the cross. Christ came in humility, as a servant. Thus, Soe concluded, the basis of religious liberty

is the fact that Christ did not come in heavenly splendor and worldly majesty to subjugate any possible resistance and force all and everybody to his subjection. Christ made himself of no reputation and took upon him the form of a servant and humbled himself even unto the death of the cross.... Never did he do anything to force people into obedience and submission.[4]

Wogaman finds certain weaknesses in this approach also. First, some oppressors have held to the "spiritual freedom" and uncoercibility of human response to God. Cromwell, as cited, would "meddle with no man's conscience," but would not permit Cath-

olics to observe the Mass. Augustine, Aquinas, and the Protestant
Reformers also asserted "spiritual freedom," but they suppressed
heretics. Thus, concluded Wogaman, "the truth is that social or
political freedom is not a direct corollary to that freedom which
the Christian finds in Christ or to the general principle of the
uncoercibility of the conscience."[5]

Another approach to religious liberty based on more explicitly
Christian grounds argues from the concept of *agape* love. *Agape*
respects and seeks the highest welfare of the person. Thus it can
not coerce. It desires fellowship with the others, but it draws them
voluntarily. As the great Danish philosopher Søren Kierkegaard,
commenting on John 12:32, put it:

> Man is himself primarily and genuinely in his free choice.
> If then our Lord will *draw* people to himself, he cannot *force*
> them to surrender. For then he would not get their real selves,
> but something different. Then he would have drawn the ob-
> ject of this "drawing" in away from their own selves in such a
> way that finally he would not have them drawn, but changed
> into a kind of impersonal machinery. He would not draw
> them; he would deceive them.[6]

Even this foundation has certain cracks, however. For one thing,
Christian ethicists have not typically understood that love, in itself, is the same as social policy. Moreover, as situation ethics
has shown, love has sometimes done negative things to achieve
positive ends. It was on grounds of love, for example, that Augustine and Aquinas justified the use of force against schismatics and
heretics.

A third approach, advocated by Reinhold Niebuhr, H. Richard
Niebuhr, Paul Tillich, and Philip Wogaman, among others, argues
from the Protestant principle that nothing human, whether church
or state, can claim infallibility. On its negative side, this approach
maintains a certain skepticism toward religious claims. Although
monotheism has sometimes produced intolerance, the fault lies not
with belief in one God but with erroneous human appropriations
of that belief. Since God transcends any person, culture, or society,
none should presume to make the kind of claims to truth on which
intolerance or persecution would be based. Every claim to absolute

representation of God is idolatrous. Even the claim that Jesus is God's final self-revelation, according to this view, does not require any to say that their own understanding of this revelation is final. Jesus himself manifested a tolerant attitude. Furthermore, Paul's concept of faith seems to eliminate dogmatism.

The major problem with this approach, it has been argued, is that it reduces the Christian view to skepticism. Proponents of the approach, however, have countered with several arguments. First, it is possible to go beyond skepticism and relativism without becoming dogmatic. The Christian may consider God's self-revelation absolute and unique truth but still demand religious liberty for all. Because the Christian holds that God has disclosed God's self in Jesus Christ, this belief should not lead to Christian arrogance about perfect understanding of God. For, if God is one, then God has not limited divine revelation to one event or set of events. We may encounter God's activity anywhere. Thus Christians base their demand for religious liberty for all persons on their own absolute claim that God is at work in all persons. To deny this freedom would be not only to frustrate humankind in its efforts to make its contribution but to frustrate God's intention to communicate the divine purpose through each person. In this sense, Wogaman said, Christians *"are not so much talking about freedom of man to be or not be 'religious' as they are talking about the freedom of God. Will God be left free to speak to and through all men?"*[7]

What will disturb some still, however, is the latitude this approach offers for heresy or error. Traditionally, Roman Catholics, Orthodox, and conservative Protestants have wanted to draw clear lines of differentiation. They have stated truth in terms of propositions that, if adhered to, assured salvation. In response to this concern it may be pointed out that Christianity is not simply a doctrinal system. It is a way of life. What matters in salvation is God's grace, not doctrine.

On this basis, Wogaman has made some specific points: (1) The heretic may be more religiously alive than someone who has less concern for faith and is only indifferently orthodox. (2) Time may change our perceptions of what is true or false, and the error may be seen later as higher truth. (3) A largely erroneous view may contain germs of truth that need new emphasis, for example, the doctrine

of free will. (4) "Error may stimulate clarification of the truth."
(5) Proponents of errors may have important contributions to make
elsewhere that would be thwarted if they were prevented from
bearing witness. (6) Heresies have often reflected social concerns
that were overlooked but that have to be considered in the interest
of justice. (7) Openness to all kinds of expressions may prevent
premature consensus.[8]

The Direction of This Study

Persons concerned for religious liberty will see validity as well as
weakness in each of the approaches suggested. The challenge is
to find a strong theoretical base to assure that religious liberty will
become a practical reality.

The strength of humanistically based approaches is that they in-
variably begin with practical realities. Accordingly, they propose to
guarantee religious liberty by means of the American tradition and
constitutional authority for the separation of church and state, pluralism, and limitation of state powers. All three points are helpful
in telling how religious liberty can be conserved. The weakness of
these approaches is that pragmatic factors will not, in the long run,
provide a stable rationale that will cover changed circumstances.
This is extremely important today, for social changes occur rapidly.
The net result of an accelerated pace of change has been the break-
down of accepted norms and their replacement by more expedient
ones. Surveillance of public persons by the CIA demonstrates that
civil and religious liberty could be set aside easily in the interest of "national safety." In the last analysis, therefore, pragmatic
approaches will fail unless they are based on deeper and more
fundamental principles.

For a Christian, the fundamental principles will be found in the
three approaches examined earlier. In my mind, each of these approaches provides a valid insight that does not exclude the others.
The most viable case may be one that combines all three.

The study that follows will begin with the biblical foundations
of both intolerance and religious liberty. Why include intolerance?
Chiefly because the Scriptures and scriptural teachings have been
cited to support intolerance as well as religious liberty. The Chris-

tian's major challenge may be, as in other areas, to learn how to interpret the Scriptures properly.

Subsequent chapters will examine the growth of the doctrine of religious liberty in the minds of Christians. By speaking of "growth," I do not mean to suggest that the Scriptures do not contain an adequate base for the doctrine. The biblical teachings are adequate. What has grown has been the Christian understanding of biblical teachings.

To suggest that Christian understanding grows may surprise some. Are not the Scriptures plain enough to be properly understood? In most instances the answer is probably yes. Nevertheless, our particular cultural setting may influence our way of viewing the Bible. We translate, interpret, and apply it to suit our cultural setting. What is going on around us will affect all of these.

In the history of Christianity the cultural context was not quite right for translating the biblical concept of religious liberty until the sixteenth and seventeenth centuries. At that time God was able, to borrow William Carey's oft-quoted phrase, to break forth new light from God's Word. Before that era, some came close to modern idiom. The real breakthrough, however, came in that period of religious wars and turmoil as people grew in their appreciation of the personal worth of the individual. Even then, religious liberty became a reality first in the American colonies and then in the Bill of Rights in the American Constitution.

The historical study will be capped by an examination of the condition of religious liberty today and a statement of some fears and hopes for the future. The writings of Soviet expatriate Alexander I. Solzhenitsyn remind us starkly that, until recent remarkable events in eastern Europe shattered the hegemony of communism, over half the world's populace has been denied religious as well as other basic freedoms. Yet fears about the fate of this basic human right must not focus on communist countries alone. Many Western countries have chosen or fallen prey to fascisms that are scarcely more tolerant of religious freedom than communism. Even democratic nations face a crisis. Growth of populations, complexities of needs, social and governmental crises, and many other factors encourage centralization of government and restriction of dissent. The development of technology has enabled governments and other social groups to mold even the conscience of human beings in a way never before conceivable. Very subtly, Christian liberty to witness may be lost not so much from direct restriction as from indirect formation by television and advertising.

Our hopes for the future of religious liberty, therefore, lie in our vigilance. It is essential that we understand well these principles that underlie this important doctrine and test practice by the principles. Erosion of religious liberty, as of any liberty, takes place almost imperceptibly. Unless a people are vigilant, they may find themselves without the cherished freedom their faith demands.

For Further Reading

Carrillo de Albornoz, Angel Francisco. *The Basis of Religious Liberty*. New York: Association Press, 1963.
Littell, Franklin H. *Christianity and Freedom*. Wilberforce, Ohio: Payne Theological Seminary, 1966.
Wogaman, Philip. *Protestant Faith and Religious Liberty*. Nashville: Abingdon Press, 1967.

For Review

1. Review the reasons for using a historical approach.

2. Discuss the meaning of religious liberty.

3. Differentiate religious liberty from liberty of conscience. What other elements does it involve?

4. Review the six approaches to religious liberty summarized in this chapter.

5. Discuss the interrelationship of the two sets of approaches. Which order would you follow in seeking to conserve religious liberty? Why?

Notes

1. A. F. Carrillo de Albornoz, *The Basis of Religious Liberty* (New York: Association Press, 1963), pp. 35–41.

2. Philip Wogaman, *Protestant Faith and Religious Liberty* (Nashville: Abingdon Press, 1967).

3. Ibid., p. 58.

4. Niels H. Soe, "The Theological Basis of Religious Liberty," *Ecumenical Review* 11, no. 1 (1958): 40.

5. Wogaman, *Protestant Faith and Religious Liberty*, pp. 58–69.

6. In Soe, "Theological Basis of Religious Liberty," p. 41.

7. Wogaman, *Protestant Faith and Religious Liberty*, p. 135. Italics his.

8. Ibid., pp. 136–42.

Chapter 2

Watch Those Scriptures!

RELIGIOUS LIBERTY rests on biblical foundations. Although other factors have furnished a place of birth, its parents were religious groups nurtured on the Bible.

Christianity's detractors have seen much irony in this fact. They have pointed out that intolerance has rested on the same biblical foundations as religious liberty. Most of the persecutors of Christian history have quoted the Scriptures and biblical teachings. They have cited God's justice and honor, love of God and neighbor, and spiritual concern as reasons for the use of force.

Because the Bible has been used in contradictory ways, it will be helpful to examine its usage in detail at one or two points. Under this concern, this chapter will trace the history of interpretation of two parables, one used in support of persecution and the other in support of toleration and freedom. This sketch, which owes much to the more detailed treatment of Frederick A. Norwood's *Strangers and Exiles*, will prepare the way for a more balanced interpretation in chapter 3.

The Great Banquet (Luke 14:15–24)

The parable of the great banquet, especially the words "Compel people to come in" in Luke 14:23, has been used since the time of Augustine as a license for persecution. The original parable was undoubtedly Jesus' reply to those who criticized his mission to the outcasts of Jewish society. The host first invited the socially respectable, but they rejected the invitation with various excuses (as the religious leaders rejected Jesus). The host then sent his servant to invite the poor and maimed and blind and lame from the city's streets (as Jesus invited outcasts). They accepted.

Matthew's account ended there (Matt. 22:10). Luke's, however, added words clearly intended to imply an invitation to the Gentiles. Since there was still room, the host instructed the servant, "Go out into the roads and lanes, and compel people to come in, so that my house may be filled. For I tell you, none of those who were invited will taste my banquet" (Luke 14:23–24 NRSV). Some scholars have questioned whether Jesus himself could have spoken these words, since Matthew did not include them in his record. If Jesus did speak them, he cannot have meant "use physical force." Such an interpretation conflicts with his attitude toward violence.

Before the time of Constantine's conversion to Christianity, no Christian thought to apply the word "compel" in the sense of forcing conversions. Christians were aggressively missionary, but they were not in a position to employ political or military force to win converts.

It was in the favorable era after Constantine adopted Christianity that Augustine, bishop of Hippo in North Africa, initiated a long history of using Luke 14:23 in justification of persecution.[1] Even for him, this application represented a change of attitude. In a letter he explained that at one time he had opposed the use of force in matters of faith. What caused him to change his mind was a discovery that force worked! His scriptural justification, however, came from Luke 14:23. In his treatise *On the Correction of Donatists*, Augustine took pains to emphasize that the Lord at first directed that the servant invite and then that he *compel*.

Later, in a letter to Donatus, Augustine differentiated between the invitation and the compulsion in terms of earlier and later times of the church. Earlier the church could not use force; in his day it could. Now that the church had strength, it must compel people to participate in the "feast of everlasting salvation." The sheep may not want to come; but once it does, it feeds contentedly in the pastures to which it was compelled.[2]

Not everyone in Augustine's day agreed with his interpretation. Augustine's own teacher, Ambrose of Milan, avoided any suggestion of compulsion in his interpretations of Luke 14:23.[3] John Chrysostom, bishop of Constantinople and one of the famous preachers of his day, rejected the idea of compelling persons to assent.[4]

Augustine's view tended to prevail in both the Roman Catholic Church of the Middle Ages and in Protestantism. Exceptions could be found, but his interpretation dominated the Middle Ages. One exception was Bernard of Clairvaux, inspiring spirit of the medieval Cistercian order. Contrary to those who would resort to force in correcting heretics, he insisted that they "be captured not by arms but by arguments." Only if they threatened to lead many others astray should force be used.[5]

More customary was Thomas Aquinas's position. In a section of his famous *Summa Theologica* he considered whether unbelievers must be compelled to believe.[6] Against compulsion he cited the parable of the tares (Matt. 13:24–30) and other authorities based upon it. Then he cited the parable of the great banquet. Those who have never received the faith should not be compelled, he argued; but even they must be coerced if they impede the faith with blasphemies, malicious debates, or open persecutions. Heretics and apostates, on the other hand, must be compelled physically "to fulfill what they promised and to hold fast to what they once received." This type of thinking justified the Inquisition, which was formally established in 1232.

One would expect the Protestant Reformers to have altered the story. Alas! They did not. Except for Martin Luther in the years before the German peasant revolt of 1523, the major Reformers uniformly cited Luke 14:23 in support of coercion. Even Luther quoted the text in favor of compulsion during the peasant revolt and afterward. John Calvin did not hesitate to draw out the literal implications of Luke 14:23. God invites, then entreats, and then "compels us by threatenings to draw near to him."[7]

The bloody persecutions and battles that accompanied the Catholic-Protestant confrontation in the sixteenth and seventeenth centuries inspired some mighty blows against the Augustinian interpretation. Sebastian Castellio wrote a defense of religious liberty. The Lucan text "Compel them to come in," he asserted, means not with a literal sword but with "the sword of the Spirit."[8] The Enlightenment of the seventeenth century carried such thinking further. When French Catholics sustained the persecution of Protestants by Louis XIV after the revocation of the Edict of Nantes in 1685, Pierre Bayle, a Huguenot (French Protestant), devoted an entire treatise to the proper exposition of Luke 14:23. His thesis was that "there is nothing more abominable than to make conversions by force."[9]

The perverse use of Scriptures may always have representatives, but the combined forces of Pietism and Puritanism all but sounded the death knell in the eighteenth century. The founder of German Pietism, Philip Jacob Spener, contended that opponents should be won by love rather than by force.[10] Following in his train, John Wesley spoke for many in his day when he insisted that his followers overwhelm opponents "with all the violence of love, and the force of God's word. Such compulsion, and such only, in matters of religion, was used by Christ and his apostles."[11]

The Tares (Matt. 13:24-30)

Just as the parable of the great banquet has served persecutors, so the parable of the tares has served defenders of religious liberty as a proof text. "Let them grow" is the opposite of "compel them to come in." Persecutors, however, have exercised considerable ingenuity to explain away the obvious import of these words.

The parable of the tares was originally Jesus' warning against trying to force the kingdom. Like the parables of the mustard seed and the leaven, it emphasized that God sets the schedule. Human beings must wait upon God to bring God's will to pass. They should exercise patience.

The complexity of the parable itself, as well as the explanation contained in Matthew 13:36-43, has resulted in several different applications. Rationalists have emphasized lack of knowledge to distinguish between wheat and tares. Others have stressed that God will one day decide. Still others have taken a legalistic approach, observing that Christ commanded tolerance. Finally, some have explained its implications away. Jesus was talking about discipline within the church, not about treatment of heretics. Thus it would not exclude persecution at all.

In the period before Constantine, the parable was usually applied to moral offenders. Normally it was cited by persons who took a more lenient view of discipline. That seems to have been the view of Matthew's Gospel. Christians should not try to distinguish bad and good too precisely. God would take care of that in the final judgment. After Matthew, the next person to apply the parable along these lines was Callistus, bishop of Rome from 217 to 222 C.E. Callistus favored the restoration of Christians, after suitable displays of repentance, who had committed adultery or fornication. In support of his position he cited the passage about the keys (Matt. 16:19), the story of Noah's ark, and the parable of the tares.[12]

After the conversion of Constantine, massive conversions caused an increase in the number of "tares" within the church. Some maintained the rigorist stance. Jerome, the greatest biblical scholar of his day and translator of the Vulgate, refuted a purist named Lucifer of Cagliari by citing the story of Noah's ark and the parable of the tares. "No one can take to himself the prerogative of Christ and judge people before the day of judgment," he insisted. "If the church is purified now, what will be left for the Lord?"[13]

Augustine developed a similar argument against the Donatists, a North African sect that fancied themselves as a "pure church," composed of "wheat" only, and thought Catholics were "tares" only. First, he denied their claim of perfection. Some Donatists operated as guerrillas, defacing Catholic churches and injuring other Christians. "Do you call these wheat?" Augustine wanted to know. Next, he contended that not all Catholics were "tares." The Catholics in North Africa cannot have become so corrupted that some wheat would not remain. At any rate, God alone will have to decide between tares and wheat, he said.

Although Augustine repudiated the Donatist contention, he did not think the parable excluded all church discipline. Jesus prohibited pulling up the tares lest the wheat also be uprooted. This means, Augustine went on to conclude, that "when the offense is public and universally condemned, bereft of defenders or at least of any who would secede, then the severity of discipline must not sleep."[14]

In the post-Constantinian era the application of the word "tares" to heresy became more or less standard. Although Jerome applied the parable to moral delinquents in one place, he applied it to heretics in another. Jerome, however, would be tolerant, "since he who is today depraved by noxious doctrine tomorrow may turn and begin to defend the truth." We must take care "where the case is dubious." We can rest assured in the fact that heretics and hypocrites will be punished in the end.[15]

John Chrysostom, who was noted for his tolerance toward non-Christians, likewise applied the parable to heretics. The parable, he concluded, prohibits slaying or killing heretics for two reasons: (1) you may also slay the saints at the same time; (2) many of the tares may change and become wheat. However, it "does not therefore forbid us to restrain heretics, to stop their mouths, to take away their freedom of speech, to break up their assemblies and societies."[16]

During the Middle Ages, the parable had applications similar to those of the earlier period. Wazo, bishop of Luik, answered an inquiry by another bishop who had asked him how he should treat heretics in his district. Citing the words, "Let both grow together until the harvest," he warned that human beings must not usurp God's role as judge. Even God spares persons in order that they may turn to God. God wants preachers to show patience too "since those who are tares today may be wheat tomorrow."[17] Bishops are not ordained to exercise secular power. They can excommunicate, but they "have no right to persecute."

The typical interpretation of the Middle Ages fell on the other side. As noted in the first section of this chapter, Thomas Aquinas harmonized conflicting attitudes toward compulsion in religion in support of the Inquisition of his day. Once more he relied on Augustine, who had argued that a moral offender could be rooted out if clearly distinguishable. Aquinas argued the same for the heretic.

The Protestant Reformation did not achieve an about-face in the use of this parable any more than it did in the use of the parable of the great banquet. The major Reformers applied it almost exactly as Thomas Aquinas did. The early Luther was an exception. Before 1528, being himself harassed by Catholics, he penned commendable pleas for religious liberty based on the parable of the tares. Christ openly commanded that the "tares," that is, heretics, be left alone. Their conversion is possible only if they are left alone. That is why Christ commanded it.[18]

The later Luther, however, reversed himself after 1528 as problems plagued his movement. Catholics cited the parable in defense of continuing their customs. Against this Luther contended that they interpreted falsely. A few years later he approved the death penalty for blasphemy, citing Augustine's change of mind regarding persecution of Donatists. He proceeded to interpret the parable to suit his new view. First, he said, the parable referred only to moral offenses. Thus it would say nothing about heretics. Impurity in the church is to be expected. Second, he restricted the directive to ministers. This would not exclude the use of force by magistrates. Indeed, they must cut off such dangerous offenses as heresy and incorrect church services.[19]

The spokesmen of the Reformed tradition, Zwingli and Calvin, applied the parable of the tares to moral wrongs. Calvin chided the Anabaptists for their rigorous discipline. They excommunicated people even for involuntary sins. They should pay attention to the parable's teaching.[20] At the same time, Calvin had to take another route when it came to justification of the burning of Michael Servetus in 1553. In this case he demanded a looser interpretation. Too rigid an interpretation would bind the magistrate and prohibit all church discipline.[21]

Some radical Reformers, especially those who sought to inaugurate the millennial reign of Christ by revolution, also reversed the intent of the parable. For these people, the end time was present, so there need be no delay in application. Thus Thomas Muntzer, a leader in the peasants' revolt, declared: "The tares must be rooted out of the vineyard of the Lord in the time of the harvest. Then the fair red wheat will take firm root."[22]

The proper significance of the parable was recovered by Christian humanists such as Erasmus, Sebastian Franck, and Sebastian Castellio. Erasmus refused to concede to complaints of scholars at the University of Paris that his view would open the way to scandal. He would not explain away the meaning of Christ's words by any of their artifices, namely, saying that the tares should be left only until the church became powerful enough to uproot them safely when Constantine became a Christian.[23]

Franck and Castellio followed in Erasmus's footsteps. Castellio contended that "tares" meant not moral offenders but heretics. They must be left alone because human beings do not know enough to sort them out. Those who have killed saints, he charged, always believed they were right.[24]

A More Excellent Way

The brief review of the use of two parables illustrates the flaws in the proof-texting method. First, one or two isolated texts do not lay down an adequate base for understanding the teaching of Scriptures on a particular subject. If one handles interpretation in this way, one usually can find a second text that stands in opposition or raises additional problems. A single text may summarize a biblical teaching in its essence. When in rare instances it does, however, it will require firmer support from the essential message of the Scriptures.

Second, disputed texts cancel each other out, and thus one has to be explained away. Here is where distortion enters the picture. The winner in disputed cases is never the texts of Scripture. Rather, it will be the prejudices of the interpreter. The interpreter will devise a method to safeguard a prejudiced view.

In the case of the parables cited here, those who favored the use of force to compel belief insisted on literal application of "compel them to come in" and on free application of "let them grow until the end." The result was a highly contradictory and contrived method of interpretation. By this convenient method, one could prove anything.

Is there a more reliable method? Because the Scriptures have been interpreted and applied in contradictory ways on this subject, some persons have said no. They have chosen instead to argue from rationalistic or humanistic principles.

Such a rejection is understandable in view of what has occurred, but it ignores the fact that Christians have an alternative to proof texting. The alternative is to set religious liberty on the deep foundations of biblical teachings about the nature of God and humankind. Admittedly, there may be dispute about these teachings too, especially if constructed by stacking proof texts on top of one another. Individual texts or even individual writings may differ on details. Moreover, the New Testament obviously goes beyond the Old Testament. Taken as a whole, however, the Scriptures present a consistent picture of God and humankind that can provide a true perspective on religious liberty.

The warp and woof of the whole tapestry is *agape* love. Although even this central concept of New Testament teaching has been subjected to contradictory uses, these uses have originated only in the most perverse kind of logic. They were not a result of failing to understand the Scriptures.

For Further Reading

Norwood, Frederick A. *Stranger and Exiles: A History of Religious Refugees.* 2 vols. Nashville: Abingdon Press, 1969. See vol. 1, pp. 59–83.

For Review

1. Read and interpret Luke 14:15–24. Check your interpretation in a commentary, such as *The Broadman Bible Commentary*, vol. 9, or in Joachim Jeremias, *The Parables of Jesus* (New York: Charles Scribner's Sons, 1963).

2. Read and interpret Matthew 13:24–30. Check your interpretation as in question 1.

3. In light of modern interpretation, discuss and evaluate the interpretations and applications reviewed in this chapter.

4. As you review the interpretations in this chapter, try to discover what led particular interpreters to their conclusions. Was it a sound method of interpretation? Was it personal prejudice? Was it the time and context in which they lived?

5. Brainstorm with your discussion group about the proper approach to the Scriptures. How do you avoid distortion? How do you assure that you are building on a solid foundation?

Notes

1. Augustine, Ep. 93, to Vincentius (408).
2. Augustine, Ep. 173, to Donatus (416).
3. Ambrose, *Two Books concerning Repentance*, 7; *Exposition of the Gospel according to Luke.*
4. Chrysostom, *Homily II on 1 Cor. 1:4–5.*
5. Bernard of Clairvaux, *Sermons on the Song of Songs*, 64, 65.
6. Thomas Aquinas, *Summa Theologica*, part II, question X, art. 8.
7. John Calvin, *Commentary on a Harmony of the Evangelists*, II, 170ff.
8. Sebastian Castellio, *Concerning Heretics*, p. 246.
9. Pierre Bayle, *Philosophical Commentary on the Words of Jesus Christ* (1686); Oeuvres diverses, 2:355–496.
10. Philip Jacob Spener, *Pia Desideria*, trans. Theodore G. Tappert (Philadelphia: Fortress Press, 1964), pp. 97–102.
11. John Wesley, *Explanatory Notes upon the New Testament*, 2d ed. (New York: Ezekiel Cooper and John Wilson, 1806), 1:186.
12. Hippolytus, *Refutation*, 9.8.
13. *Dialogue against the Luciferians*, 22; PL 23:186.
14. *Against the Letter of Parmenian*, III, 2, 13; CSEL 51:115.
15. *Commentary on the Gospel of Matthew*, II, 13.
16. *Homilies on Matthew*, 46; PG 58:477; NPNF 10:289.
17. Paul Fredericq, *Corpus Documentorum Inquisitionis Haereticae*, I, 6–7; cited by Frederick A. Norwood, *Strangers and Exiles: A History of Religious Refugees* (Nashville: Abingdon Press, 1969), 1:76.
18. Martin Luther, *Fastenpostille*, 1525; *Werke*, XVII 2, 125.
19. Ibid., 52:831, 835, 836, 838.
20. John Calvin, "Brief Instruction against the Anabaptists," *Corpus Reformatorum*, Calvini Opera, 8:74.
21. John Calvin, "Refutation of the Errors of Michael Servetus," *Corpus Reformatorum*, 8:472.
22. Thomas Muntzer, cited by Norwood, *Strangers and Exiles*, 1:83.
23. Erasmus, *Declaration of Erasmus to the Censures of the Theology Faculty of Paris*, 74.
24. Castellio, *Against Calvin's Book*; cited by Norwood, *Strangers and Exiles*, 1:83.

Chapter 3

Scriptural Seed

THE HISTORICAL REVIEW of the preceding chapter flashes a caution light for one trying to discover a biblical basis for religious liberty. Contradictory interpretations and applications of the Scriptures have led some to sweep away this basis and construct a totally humanistic one.

Although a Christian must concede that one can approach religious liberty by other paths, appreciation of the Bible as divine revelation will hardly allow us to neglect it in discussing doctrine. Even if religious liberty was not begotten in the biblical era, its seed was there. The challenge is to see the small seed nestled in the womb, ready to be brought forth when it reached full term.

I will argue that the sources of religious liberty reside in monotheism, in the nature of God as love, and in the New Testament understanding of the distinction between civil and religious authority. Each of these has been used, but surely in perverse ways, to justify persecution. Seen in their fully developed form, especially in the teachings of Jesus and the early church, they provide fertile seed for a modern understanding of religious liberty.

God of All Nations

A Christian rationale for religious liberty should begin with the foundational doctrine of belief in one God. Such an approach is essential because many proponents of religious liberty have ascribed intolerance and persecution to this doctrine. The charge, unfortunately, has substance. However, those who have inferred intolerance from monotheism have not looked closely enough at its implications. A concept of God as a tribal or national deity has prevailed over a concept of God as the God of all persons, equally concerned for all and revealing God's self to all.

Particular Monotheism and Intolerance

The crucial question is whether monotheists can be tolerant, conscious of the right of all persons to choose their own religion. Many will say no. Monotheism produces proselytism. All who proselytize are intolerant and do not respect the liberty of others. They may harass and persecute other persons.

Anyone who knows the history of Israel, Christianity, and Islam can cite evidence to support this line of reasoning. The Old Testament abounds in illustrations of intolerance, persecutions, and crusades. What kind of belief produced these? Was it monotheism in itself? Or was it monotheism of an erroneous and perverse sort?

Since a monotheistic religion had much to do with the development of genuine religious liberty, it was surely the latter. It was essentially a particularistic monotheism that viewed God as a tribal deity limited by space and time. God was Israel's God. God favored no other peoples.

The conquest of the land of Canaan should be seen in this light. Essentially it was a crusade. It was a crusade in which Israel could act without mercy against the enemy, wiping out men, women, and children as they went (see Josh. 6:21; 8:24–26). To protect the people of Israel from Canaanite influences, particularistic rules were laid down. These rules often prescribed rigorous penalties for having any contacts with foreigners. Such nationalistic intolerance reached its peak expression in Old Testament books such as Esther and Obadiah and in inter-testamental writings such as 1 Maccabees. Jesus described much of the Old Testament when he said, " You have heard that it was said, "You shall love your neighbor and hate your enemy' " (Matt. 5:43, NRSV).

This particularism was attached to the covenant concept. God was Israel's God. Israel was to be God's people, unique among all nations. "Jacob I loved, but Esau I hated!" (see Mal. 1:2–3.)

There is no denying the existence of this kind of monotheism. It fed not only Israel but, during many centuries, the Christian church. The issue is: Is it the *only* kind of monotheism? Or did another kind of monotheism exist alongside it that could eventually give birth to tolerance and even religious liberty?

Universal Monotheism and Religious Liberty

The Old Testament contains at least the beginnings of such a monotheism. It was the same universalistic monotheism that gave rise to the Jewish and then to the Christian mission. This monotheism began with Abraham. As he departed from Ur, the father of the Hebrews broke away from the idea that God dwells only in temples made by human hands. God met him wherever he went, and he proceeded with faith that God would do so. Abraham came close to true monotheism in the covenant he made with God. By this covenant he was to go to a land God would show him. In return God would make of him "a great nation" and bless him and make his name great, so that he would "be a blessing" and by him "all the families of the earth" would bless themselves (see Gen. 12:1–3). The important thing about this covenant insofar as religious liberty is concerned was Abraham's discovery that God had a *universal* concern. God would bless not Abraham alone but *all* peoples. That concern should be the foundation not of intolerance but of complete liberty.

Despite lapses from the Abrahamic covenant, monotheism not only survived but ultimately developed into the universal monotheism of Jesus. The next step came in the Mosaic covenant. Although this covenant possibly opened the way to intolerance in some respects, it reasserted the insights of the Abrahamic covenant. On the side of intolerance, the covenant set particularistic requirements. Most of the instructions were addressed to the covenant people alone and to those living within their territory. Moreover, the covenant did not keep Israel from mounting a campaign to drive the Canaanites from their homes in order to establish themselves in the promised land. The conquest of Canaan represents a narrowing of monotheism. The people of Israel did not envision God as having concern for all peoples.

Some essential features of the covenant, however, stand against the particularistic, narrow view represented here. The underlying condition of the covenant was that if Israel would obey God's voice and keep the covenant, they would be God's " 'treasured possession out of all the peoples' " and " 'a priestly kingdom and a holy nation' " (Ex. 19:5–6, NRSV). This condition made the right deduction from belief in one God: God is concerned for all the peoples of the earth, and God had chosen Israel for a priestly ministry to them, not for dominance over them.

Although for centuries particularism prevailed over universalism in interpretations of the monotheistic covenant, breakthroughs did occur. In the seventh century B.C.E. Isaiah envisioned a day when God would say, " 'Blessed be Egypt my people, and Assyria the work of my hands,' " as well as " 'Israel my heritage' " (Isa. 19:25, NRSV). Alongside hatred of Edomites, Malachi put a beautiful vision of God's universal concern: "For from the rising of the sun to its setting my name is great among nations, and in every place incense is offered to my name, and a pure offering; for my name is great among nations, says the Lord of hosts' " (Mal. 1:11, RSV).

For the period after the Exile, the most significant breakthrough may have been made by the author of Isaiah 40–55. Although scholars debate how universalist the writer was, it is highly significant for his understanding of God that he believed God had chosen Cyrus, the Medo-Persian king, as God's anointed. God directed not merely the events of Israel's history but the events of all history. Further, this prophet reminded Israel that God had a universal concern of which Israel was not the goal but the instrument.

The famous Servant poems (Isa. 42:1–4; 49:1–6; 50:4–9; 52:13–53:12) reflect a universal purpose involving all nations. God had chosen the Servant to "bring forth justice to the nations," and the Servant would not stop until "he has established justice in the earth" (42:1,4, NRSV). It was not enough for the Servant to restore Israel. Rather, God would give him " 'as a light to the nations, that my salvation may reach to the end of the earth' " (49:6, NRSV). The Servant would "startle many nations" (52:15, NRSV).

The mission, therefore, was universal. God wished to extend salvation to the ends of the earth. What about religious liberty?

On this question the crucial issue seemed to be one of method: How was the mission to be achieved? Here the answer was seldom supportive of tolerance. On the contrary, the extension of God's name would take place through vindication of God's people. The more politically oppressed the Hebrew people were, the stronger the expressions of vengeance.

Ezra and Nehemiah, after the Exile, heightened the exclusive features of the covenant in restoration of the Temple and elevation of the Law to a place of absolute significance. During the era of Greek rule, the Maccabees stiffened opposition to Greek customs and engaged in a vigorous war against Greek rule. The Essenes, who probably originated during the same era, believed that God had called them to prepare for the battle when God would at last vanquish the enemies of God's people. This would be the battle of God's people against Satan's people, "the time of salvation for the people of God, the critical moment when those who have cast their lot with Him will come to dominion, whereas those that have cast it with Belial shall be doomed to eternal extinction."[1] In 68 C.E., sure that God's angels would join them in the fray, the Essenes engaged in battle with the Romans, believing the battle of Armageddon had begun. They were wiped out.

Jesus' Monotheism and Religious Liberty

The Jewish people grasped to some degree the implications of monotheism for mission, but they did not grasp its significance for tolerance. On the contrary, the mission was thought of in terms of vengeance. It remained for early Christianity to break through here with the insight that "God is no respecter of persons" (see Acts 10:34; Rom. 2:11; Eph. 6:9; Col. 3:25; Jas. 2:1). God manifests saving love to anyone God chooses, as and where God chooses.

1. Jesus removed the idea of national vengeance from the Jewish hope. The clearest example of this is found in Jesus' attitude toward Samaritans. He healed a Samaritan along with Jewish lepers (Luke 17:11–19), upheld a Samaritan as an example of compassion (Luke 10:25–37), and condemned the hostile attitude of his disciples to the Samaritans (Luke 9:51–55). In quoting the words of Isaiah 61:2 in his synagogue sermon at Capernaum, he left out words about vengeance (Luke 4:16–19).

2. Jesus promised the Gentiles a share in salvation. Gentiles —
the Ninevites and the Queen of Sheba (Matt. 12:41–42; Luke
11:21–23), inhabitants of Tyre and Sidon (Matt. 11:22; Luke 10:14),
and even inhabitants of Sodom and Gomorrah (Matt. 10:15; Luke
10:12) — would participate in the resurrection. Both Jews and Gentiles would be present at the final judgment (Matt. 25:31–46). Some
Gentiles would "inherit the kingdom" (Matt. 25:34). Some Jews,
unless they repented, would be excluded from the kingdom (Matt.
8:11–12: Luke 13:28–30). Indeed, God had shown such judgment
by sending Elijah only to a Gentile widow and commanding Elisha
to heal only the Syrian leper Naaman (Luke 4:25–26).

3. Jesus' own redemptive activity included Gentiles. The resolution of what appears to be somewhat contradictory views
undoubtedly lies, as Professor Jeremias pointed out, in Jesus' belief that beyond the cross God would gather all the nations to the
holy mountain. Remarking about the faith of the Roman centu-
rion who sent to him to have his servant healed, he said: " 'Truly,
I tell you, in no one in Israel have I found such faith. I tell you,
many will come from east and west and will eat with Abraham
and Isaac and Jacob in the kingdom of heaven, while the heirs of
the kingdom will be thrown into the outer darkness' " (Matt. 8:10–
12, NRSV).[2] Here at last was a universal monotheism that could
serve as a base for both the universal mission of Christianity and
genuine religious liberty. Some implications for the latter need to
be spelled out.

First, Jesus' teaching emphasized God's universal concern. God
is not the God of the Jews alone but the God of all peoples.

Second, his view implies that God alone has the final say about a
person's allegiance to God. God alone can discern whether human
belief or commitment suffices to please God. No one will know
until the final judgment who belongs to the sheep and who to the
goats.

Third, his view implies that no one should be so presumptu-
ous as to usurp God's right and authority to decide. Coercion in
religious matters would be the ultimate presumption. It assumes
that one person can look into another's heart in the way God does
and render a final judgment before the time. As Jesus' criticisms
of the religious leaders of his day indicate, God never surrenders
that right.

If these conclusions are correct, then, fourth, the attracting of persons to faith and discipleship can involve only voluntary methods of persuasion. Christians announce God's message. They urge persons to respond. They call them to join the people of God. But they cannot *coerce* anyone to respond. It is, as Luther pointed out in his early days as a reformer, the Word of God that must bring assent. "I will preach it, teach it, write it," he said in a sermon at Wittenberg in 1522, "but I will constrain no one by force, for faith must come freely without compulsion."

Early Christianity's Monotheism and Religious Liberty

Jesus freed monotheism and mission from Jewish particularism and, with that, from intolerance. His insight, however, remained to be implemented by early Christianity. Luke-Acts and Paul's letters especially tell the story of the breakout of Christianity from Jewish particularism to genuine universalism. This universalism is well summed up in Peter's words about the conversion of Cornelius and his household in Acts 10:34–35 (RSV): " 'Truly I perceive that God shows no partiality, but in every nation any one who fears him and does what is right is acceptable to him.' "

To many Christians this statement implies *too* much. It makes no mention of faith in Christ. That Luke did not intend to omit this faith is made clear in what follows, as also in Acts 4:12 " 'And there is salvation in no one else, for there is no other name under heaven given among human beings by which we must be saved.' " The one God had revealed God's self in a particular way in Jesus, Israel's Messiah. It is in him, therefore, that "There is no longer Jew and Greek, . . . slave or free, . . . male and female" (Gal. 3:28, NRSV).

If Christians make such a claim for the finality of God's self-disclosure in Christ, do they not immediately recreate the motive for intolerance and persecution? Can they say "there is no other name" and "he is the way" without endangering the liberty of others?

Subsequent chapters will point up the real dangers here. Christians often have become so convinced that they possessed the final truth that they have not stopped at violent coercion to make converts. The earliest Christians, however, did not go so far. They maintained a taut line between zeal to share the good news of

God's disclosure in Jesus of Nazareth and recognition that belief must be voluntary. Where was the line? What drew it for them?

Almost certainly it derived from their recognition that God is the ultimate, sole judge of human response. Human beings are at best instruments in God's plan. They can make only modest claims about evoking faith in God from their fellow human beings. Whatever means they employ, they can never determine the results.

Witness what Paul had to say about the Corinthian mission. What are Apollos and Paul? he asked. Nothing but "servants through whom you came to believe, as the Lord assigned to each. I planted, Apollos watered, but God gave the growth. So neither the one who plants nor the one waters is anything, but only God who gives the growth" (1 Cor. 3:5–7, NRSV). This agrees exactly with Jesus' parables about the mustard seed and the leaven (Mark 4:30–32; Matt. 13:31–33; Luke 13:18–21). God alone decrees how God's reign will grow. Human beings may announce it. They may urge others to enter. They cannot determine who does enter.

This being so, human beings cannot set boundaries for God's rule, whether boundaries of creed or custom. God's rule involves a personal relationship to God. God may establish this personal relationship with anyone God chooses on any conditions God chooses. Thus, according to the story of the early Christian mission presented in Acts, God did not accept circumcision and obedience to Jewish ritual laws as a condition for salvation of the Gentiles. God set only the condition of personal faith in Jesus Christ as Lord (Acts 2:38; 8:16; 11:17). Even this, however, could not be coerced. The Spirit, God personally present, alone determined the authenticity of response.

Love Constrains Us

Monotheism, properly interpreted, may serve as the motive for both the Christian mission and religious liberty. More needs to be said, however, about the nature of God as reflected in the Scriptures. Here, too, the picture is blurred if one does not recognize development in biblical understanding. By certain Old Testament texts, interpreted literally, God appears chiefly as lawgiver and judge, harsh and vindictive in nature, demanding things of human beings that conflict with what we know of God's self-disclosure in Christ.

"God Is Love"

In the terse statement "God is love," the author of 1 John (4:8) summed up the deepest insight of the Christian faith. That insight had been building. But until John said it, no one phrased it with such precision. The Jews knew God's covenant love or mercy. They experienced God's long-suffering or patience over centuries of faithfulness and unfaithfulness. Hosea pictured this love best in his long-suffering toward his unfaithful wife, Gomer. It was the experience of God's love in Jesus, however, that brought the picture into focus.

In his epochal study *Agape and Eros*, Anders Nygren has listed four features of *agape* love. First, it is spontaneous or self-motivated. It has its source in God (1 John 4:7). Unlike the love of a more human sort, *eros*, it is not drawn magnet-like by the attraction of another person. It loves the other because love belongs to its very essence.

Second, because it is self-originating, it does not play favorites. God "makes his sun rise on the evil and on the good, and sends rain on the righteous and on the unrighteous" (Matt. 5:45, NRSV). God accepts the rejects and the outcasts of society. Like the loving father in the parable of the prodigal, God throws aside all dignity to welcome the son who strayed (Luke 15:20–24). Then, ultimately, "God proves his love for us in that while we still were sinners Christ died for us" (Rom. 5:8, NRSV). Love can do nothing greater than to lay down its life (John 15:13).

Third, love creates value in that which it loves. Human beings try to shape others in their mold. *Agape* love, however, does not compel change; it creates merit. Thus those who were without merit have become precious. Love renews and transforms.

Fourth, *agape* love is the initiator of fellowship with God. It is God's way to humankind, not humankind's way to God. "In this is love, not that we loved God but that he loved us and sent his Son to be the atoning sacrifice for our sins" (1 John 4:10, NRSV). We would not know love unless God first loved us (1 John 4:19).

Agape *Love and Coercion*

The implications of *agape* love for religious liberty may seem self-evident. It may come as a surprise, then, that Christians have cited love as the motive for compulsion. Augustine's argument in a letter to Boniface, an official of the Roman province of Africa, represents the first and most influential example.

It was Augustine's contention that love would compel pagans, heretics, and schismatics to join the church. In support of this thesis, he noted first that love is the motive for the Christian mission. He proceeded from that argument to his major one. Love will use whatever means are needed to achieve the greater good for a person. Physicians, for example, will do things that pain their patients, but they do so for a long-range good. The patients may complain. Later, however, they will recognize the love involved and return the physicians' love. Augustine refused to yield to the Donatist claim that they were the true church because of persecution by Catholics. Neither does being persecuted prove that Catholics are wrong. Motive is what counts here.

No one, for example, would hesitate to force another person from a burning building against his or her will. To leave someone there to die would be sadistic. It is the function of brotherly love to rescue that person. By analogy, no one should hesitate to help another escape the fires of hell, even if force were needed. For love "ardently desires that all should live, but it more especially labors that not all should die."[3]

Even Christ, the ultimate exemplar of love, used force in the conversion of Paul. Not only did he constrain him with his voice, "but even dashed him to the earth with his power."[4] If force worked to such advantage in this case, Augustine argued, why should the church not use force? This is a matter of saving someone about to commit suicide. Its motive is love.

Agape *Love and Religious Liberty*

Augustine's line of reasoning demonstrates how essential it is for Christians to balance their desire that all persons know God's truth as revealed in Jesus Christ with their recognition that the only coercion they can apply is that of reason and love. *The flaw in Au-*

gustine's reasoning is the assumption that the end justifies the means. The end, in this case, is commendable: the salvation of persons. To use force to obtain it, he thought, is also commendable. The question that must be posed is: Does love not decree the means as well as the end? I would answer emphatically yes. *Agape* love does not allow one to detach the means from the end. In their concern for the conversion of the non-Christian, Christians cannot use means that do not give the fullest attention to the latter's freedom and personal integrity. Love may reason, urge, and plead. It cannot use force. The Scriptures make clear that to apply love in this way not only usurps God's prerogative but contradicts its very nature.

Out of love, God created humanity. From the divine point of view God created humanity not because of any inherent deficiency or need of God's own but because it is love's nature to create. God did not have to, but God did. From the point of view of humanity, God created human beings to enjoy personal communion with God's self. Personal communion can be personal only when it is voluntary. Human love responds to, reciprocates, the divine love. If communion were coerced, it would cease to be communion. There might be interaction in a kind of over-under relationship, but there would not be communion. Communion, in its very nature, involves a parent-child, friend-friend exchange; there cannot be communion in a master-slave relationship. It must be voluntary.

This is why, in the Scriptures, the history of salvation is essentially a story of God's patient effort to woo errant humanity back to God's self. By virtue of the way God created humanity, God could not force communion. God created humanity free either to live in communion or not. When humanity chose not, "fell," God employed voluntary means to restore communion. God called Israel, the Old Testament story records, to be the instrument for the reconciliation of humankind. When Israel failed, God sought a remnant for the task. Finally, in Jesus of Nazareth, God left the final witness of the way love works. God would not win back errant humanity by force but by the gentle compulsion of love itself.

As Peter Abelard said during the Middle Ages, when the church often used force of arms to compel consent if not belief, the cross is the ultimate witness. For the redemption of humanity, God did not choose the way of the kings of the world — violence and power. Not even the persuasiveness of human speech or reason was used

(1 Cor. 1:18–31). God chose instead the way of the Servant, the way of the cross. When found in human form, he took upon himself the role of a servant and became obedient even to death (Phil. 2:6–11). By dying, he drew others to himself. Lifted up on the cross, he would draw all persons (John 12:32).

The New Testament also contains an element of judgment. Would not the idea of judgment allow room for coercion? If God judges, then does God not coerce? Does God not use the compulsion of fear?

The answer to these questions is yes and no. True, God does determine the final destiny of all humanity. Since God created humankind, God will decree its ultimate end. Without God humanity would never have come into being. Without God humanity would cease to be.

With reference to coercion and freedom, however, I would emphasize two things about judgment. First, throughout most of the New Testament, judgment was present in Jesus, but that was in the sense that he was a foresign of the final day (John 3:19; 5:22–29; 8:16; 12:31). A final judgment, nevertheless, awaits the end of history, when God shall have wrapped up God's purpose for humanity. Meantime, God deals patiently with humanity. God delays judgment, "not wanting any to perish but all to come to repentance" (2 Pet. 3:9, NRSV).

Second, God does not relinquish judgment to human beings. Christ may have promised his followers a share in the final judgment (Matt. 19:28), but he also reminded them that God has the final word. Before that final day, moreover, God forbade judging. Whoever takes God's judgment into their own hands can expect to be evaluated in the way they had judged others (Matt. 7:1–5; Luke 7:37–38). God alone can judge the inner person. God alone knows the heart (Ps. 7:9; 26:2; Jer. 11:20; 17:10; Rev. 2:23).

This is the crucial point that defenders of religious liberty have made repeatedly. Belief, whether right or wrong, is a personal matter. It involves not merely rational assent but an intensely personal relation between personal beings. God and the believer alone can know the integrity of this personal relationship. However intense external pressures may be, they cannot arouse love for God in the persecuted. In Jesus' parable of the last judgment, those who were invited to enter into God's kingdom did not know they had served God, whereas some who thought they had served God were rejected (Matt. 25:31–46). If we cannot have dogmatic certainty about our own relationship to God, how can we have it about our fellow human being's relationship?

"Render unto Caesar . . ."

Thus far, I have sought to lay a foundation for a doctrine of religious liberty from the perspective of an inner human liberty. Still to be constructed is a foundation from a broader perspective. What is the basis of the freedom to proclaim a message, to assemble, and to engage in corporate activities?

The Old Testament offers little help in answering this question because Israel did not differentiate between religious and civil activities. Israel was a religious state. All of its activities bore a religious nuance. The New Testament is more helpful, although no New Testament writer answered the question in terms of religious liberty as a right to be guaranteed by government. On the contrary, preaching, assembling for worship, and corporate religious activities were engaged in as acts of obedience to God. Civil authorities can regulate some activities, but they cannot control or restrict those that God decrees or inspires. In disputed cases, as the early apostles decided, "We must obey God rather than any human authority" (Acts 5:29, NRSV). Here, however, the critical issue has always been: Where is the line that separates civil matters, where human authorities merit obedience, from religious matters, where God alone merits obedience? The first Christians found the question difficult to answer.

On the one hand, converts to Christianity were taught obedience to established authority. This meant, in the first centuries of the Christian era, obedience to the Roman emperor, provincial officials, and local magistrates. Such obedience was based on a recognition that all political authority, even that which was hostile to Christianity, derives from one God (Rom. 13:1–7). God grants authority to rulers so that they may contribute to human welfare by keeping order. The Christian, therefore, should pray for all acknowledged authorities so that all persons "may lead a quiet and peaceable life" (1 Tim. 2:2). Whoever resists this authority,

Paul contended, "resists what God has appointed" and will incur judgment (Rom. 13:2, NRSV). The ruler is "God's servant for your good" and a terror only to someone doing wrong (13:4, NRSV). If any should suffer for misdeeds, they would have no cause for complaint (1 Pet. 4:15–16).

The principle laid down here left the Christian with little option. Jesus had commanded that the civil government, even an unjust one, be obeyed. When asked whether a Jew should pay the hated Roman tax, Jesus replied, "Give to the emperor the things that are the emperor's, and to God the things that are God's" (Mark 12:17, NRSV). In regard to civil affairs, as Paul summed up the same principle later, this meant, "Pay to all what is due them — taxes to whom taxes are due, revenue to whom revenue is due, respect to whom respect is due, honor to whom honor is due" (Rom. 13:7, NRSV).

Obedience to established authority, then, was the rule, for God granted and sanctioned such authority. But what about instances where civil authority stood in opposition to another clearly attested plan of God, namely, in the spread of Christianity? Should there be the same submission? Opposition of both Jewish and Roman authorities quickly put Christians on the horns of a dilemma. They wanted to obey. Yet how could they without opposing God's direct command to spread the good news? The solution lay in a distinction between the authority of the state in civil affairs and its authority in religious affairs. Regarding the former, Christians would obey the established authorities; regarding the latter, they could not.

The basis for this distinction was implicit in Jesus' reply to the Pharisees and Herodians on the tax issue. God has not granted *all* authority to the political powers. God has granted that authority necessary for civil welfare. God has reserved for God's self the authority that belongs to the religious sphere. Thus, as early Christians conceived the issue, taxes go to Caesar but worship to God alone.

If obedience in religious matters were purely a matter of conscience, a problem might not have arisen from this view. External forces may shape the conscience to some degree, but they cannot take complete control of it, although modern "psyching" or "brainwashing" techniques pose dangers to the inner self never before experienced. But worship of God is not purely a matter of conscience. It also involves proclamation of religious truths, assembling, and corporate activities that overlap the civil realm. It was in these areas that the Christians' desire to obey the authorities was severely tested. When tested, they found that in some matters they had to "obey God rather than any human authority" (Acts 5:29).

The test came from opposite sides. From one side, it involved prohibition of evangelization and winning of converts, first in Jerusalem and then elsewhere. The authorities may be forgiven in part for their attitude. In their minds Christianity threatened to disrupt the harmony of their government. To the Jews, the Christian preaching threatened the Temple and the Law, the twin pillars of their whole way of life (Acts 6:11, 14). To municipal officials in various cities, Christian missionaries were "turning the world upside down" (see Acts 17:6). Later, Roman emperors had a similar concern for the peace of the empire. Their concern was for civil order. How far could they let zealous evangelists go?

From another side, the test involved conformity to the established religious customs. Conformity was essential to the welfare of the state. This was much more the Roman than the Jewish position. Once more, however, it was not easy to distinguish civil and religious.

In the end the crucial issue is: Who shall decide where the line between civil and religious authority is drawn? Will it be the individual, the religious group to which one belongs, or government at various levels? So long as one thinks only of freedom of conscience, the question does not have to be answered. But when one thinks of public expressions of religion, it must be answered. Freedom here is never unlimited, for public expressions of religion bear upon the public domain.

Most persons in the ancient world, as perhaps in the modern, would say that civil authorities should decide what public expressions are permitted. They should do so because they have to guard the welfare of all persons within their domains. Christians, however, responded differently. The divine revelation they received in Christ gave them a mandate. They could not stop preaching, regardless of the strictures of civil authorities. To "obey God rather than any human authority" meant for them to pursue their mission as a direct commission of God.

The price of this civil disobedience was persecution. Neither Jewish nor Roman officials tolerated it for long. How did Christians view the persecution? They did not resist violently. Rather, they endured. Suffering for the Christian name made them participants in Christ's sufferings. To share in his sufferings signified a good fortune, for it prefigured their sharing in his resurrection glory (1 Pet. 4:13–16). One day, the writer of the Revelation promised, God would vindicate them. Meanwhile, they had to endure patiently.

The first Christians opted for the freedom of the individual and religious groups to express their religious faith publicly and institutionally. In doing so, they did not indicate where the lines sometimes have to be drawn to protect both individuals or religious groups in their beliefs and the body politic as a whole. People sometimes engage in hurtful activities on religious grounds. As an act of "obedience to God," for example, some have murdered. Some have taken their own lives. Some have engaged in licentious behavior. Some have disrupted the civil order. Who, then, in these cases, should draw the line? Where should the line be drawn between civil welfare and religious obedience? Obviously, no easy answer can be found. The most satisfactory answer found thus far was centuries in the making.

Conclusion

To sum up, the seed of religious liberty lay hidden in the Scriptures in universal monotheism and in *agape* love. At the same time, belief that God is the God of all persons inspired a mission to the world and laid a foundation not simply for toleration but for complete liberty. If all are to share in the salvation God offers, then there must be complete liberty to proclaim God's name to all the nations. Belief that God is disinterested love, that God plays no favorites, put its weight against coercion as a means of pursuing this mission. Faith as personal relationship cannot be coerced. It can be only voluntary.

Both monotheism and *agape* love suffered from narrowing. Belief that God is the God of all nations sometimes became belief that God is the God of a particular tribe or nation. Universal love became love of fellow Jews. As a result, the way was opened to religious pride and persecution. In Jesus of Nazareth, however, particularism gave way to true universalism. The God of all persons manifests God's love toward all. Not human beings but God will make final decisions about the salvation of humankind.

The plea of Christians for religious liberty fell mostly on deaf ears in the ancient world. Obedience to God in preaching and other religious activities evoked suppression and persecution. Through three centuries of travail, however, the seed grew in the womb. With Constantine the infant religious liberty was born, but it did not survive.

For Further Reading

Cullmann, Oscar. *The State in the New Testament*. London: SCM Press, 1957.
Nygren, Anders. *Agape and Eros*. Trans. Philip S. Watson. 2nd ed. New York: Macmillan Co., 1953.

For Review

1. Review the discussion of monotheism. Distinguish between particularistic and universal monotheism.

2. In what way is particularistic monotheism a cause of intolerance? Does this understanding of God operate in America today? Are there ways in which it may threaten religious liberty?

3. In what way is universal monotheism a basis for the Christian mission? for religious liberty?

4. Discuss the features of *agape* love. What implications have these for religious liberty?

5. Review Augustine's love argument for the use of coercion. What is the flaw in it? What kind of coercion is permissible if love guides the means of evangelism?

6. Discuss the problem of Christian obedience to civil authorities who restrict or oppose preaching, assembling, or corporate activities. Who

should decide disputed cases? The individual? a religious group? civil authorities?

7. Where would you establish a line between civil and religious responsibility?

Notes

1. *The War of the Sons of Light and the Sons of Darkness*, I, 1–17; trans. Theodor H. Gaster, *The Dead Sea Scriptures in English Translation* (Garden City, N.Y.: Doubleday and Co., 1956), p. 281.

2. Joachim Jeremias, *Jesus' Promise to the Nations*, Studies in Biblical Theology 24 (Naperville, Ill.: Alec R. Allenson, 1958).

3. *On the Correction of the Donatists*, III, 14; NPNF 4:638.

4. *On the Correction of the Donatists*, VI, 22; NPNF 4:641.

Chapter 4

The Stillbirth of Religious Liberty

RELIGIOUS LIBERTY was born in the first three centuries of Christian history, but it did not survive. Actually it was stillborn, for those who voiced eloquent pleas for their own liberty soon agreed to deny it to others. The atmosphere was not right for its survival.

In view of this tragedy one might think it unprofitable to review this segment of the story. Why worry over a corpse? Why not skip over this episode to a successful one? The answer to these questions is that we learn as much, if not more, from our failures as from our successes. As far as religious liberty is concerned, we have still to learn from the tragedies, errors, and failures of the past.

To understand why religious liberty was stillborn in this period requires an examination of its environment and ancestry as well as the mother.

Rome and Religious Liberty

The environment was the Roman Empire, a vast colossus sprawling over the Mediterranean world. Rome almost gave birth to religious liberty. Compared to other ancient peoples, the Romans were tolerant. Nevertheless, tolerance is not religious liberty. When Christianity emerged as an aggressively missionary faith, Roman tolerance proved to be thin. It quickly gave way to persecution.

Roman Tolerance

Roman tolerance, as many students of religious liberty have pointed out, was related to its polytheism. Like the Greeks, the Romans worshiped "gods many and lords many." The Roman pantheon had a place for all the gods of captive nations. It began, of course, with the ancient gods of Rome, largely ancestral deities. It incorporated the vast Greek pantheon, the Olympian gods of Homer and all the rest. Then it made room for the gods of other people, including the oriental deities. Lest they forget any, the Romans erected monuments "to unknown gods."

Roman intolerance, like that of the Greeks, arose only in connection with paying the gods their proper due. The average Roman believed that Rome had risen to power not simply because the Roman gods were more powerful than any others but also because Roman devotion to the gods was more powerful. Proper devotion was assured through observance of carefully prescribed rituals. Every citizen was bound to discharge these rituals. Performance was not optional, since the welfare of the empire depended on the right expressions of devotion.

As long as all persons fulfilled these obligations, however, they had almost complete freedom to engage in other forms of religion. Here Rome displayed remarkable tolerance.

Rome tolerated the oriental mystery religions — Mithra, Isis and Osiris, Cybele, and others. Except when Rome found some of them guilty of flagrant immoralities, it granted a free hand. Masses of Roman citizens flocked to those, finding in them satisfaction for emotional as well as intellectual needs not met by the stiff state cultus. The cults fitted well within the framework of Roman tolerance, for they too were tolerant. They allowed their members to belong to other cults. They interchanged ideas and customs freely. Thus they put no restrictions on participation in rituals required by the state.

Rome also tolerated Judaism. This toleration was based on a different rationale, however, for Judaism was not inherently tolerant like the oriental cults. The monotheism of Judaism made it exclusive, even intolerant. It did not allow its members to belong to other religions. It did not exchange ideas and customs indiscriminately with others. Rome, however, could encourage it, so long as Jews did not try to proselytize too many Romans. Proper respect to the God of the Jews by God's own people would ensure God's favor, along with that of all the other deities, toward the Roman Empire. Jews paying homage to their God made sense. Occasionally the Jews did experience the Roman lash, but not often. They were expelled from Rome in 44 C.E. by an edict of Claudius, but that probably was related to disturbance over Christianity (Acts 18:2).

Rome even tolerated skeptics. The Athenians had given Socrates the fatal hemlock for doubting the existence of the gods. The Romans, however, were more tolerant so long as none refused proper duties in the state cultus. They put no one to death for religious beliefs until Christianity appeared.

Many persons in the upper ranks of society were indifferent to religion. In the first two centuries of the Christian era, they were attracted to Stoicism. Stoicism offered an excellent moral guide, but it held a rather impersonal concept of God. Many could go through the prescribed rituals without abandoning Stoic principles. Stoics like the emperor Marcus Aurelius could not comprehend the inflexibility of Christians toward the legal requirements of the state religion.

During the second century and the early third century, a solar monotheism developed. This solar monotheism, as formulated by Plutarch, author of the famous *Lives of the Caesars*, combined many religious beliefs and customs into one hodgepodge. It combined monotheism and polytheism, the Roman state religion and the oriental cults, the philosophies and popular superstitions. Plutarch theorized a hierarchy of gods in four tiers. At the top was the supreme God, the Unconquered Sun; below him were the planetary gods; below them were the demons, the old Olympian gods; and below them were the spirits of the dead, sprites, goblins, and "things that go bump in the night." Someone had at last fashioned the ultimate synthesis of human religious experience!

About 200 C.E. Alexander Severus wanted to erect a temple to Christ and "receive him among the gods." Had he done so, the triumph of the Roman spirit would have been complete.

Roman Intolerance

Rome was remarkably tolerant, and Roman critics of Christianity were not slow to charge Christianity with intolerance. From the Roman point of view, the charge was accurate. Like its parent religion, Judaism, Christianity was a monotheistic faith. Christians, too, said, "Hear, O Israel, the Lord our God is one Lord" (Deut. 6:4). This one and only God would tolerate no competitors, whether in the state religion or in the oriental cults. Accordingly, one could not be a Christian and at the same time offer incense to the gods or the genius of the emperor or belong to one of the other sects. One could not even belong to Christianity's parent religion, Judaism, for this God had revealed God's self in a definitive way in Jesus, Israel's Messiah. Christianity developed a sophisticated formation process whereby its converts would pledge ultimate and exclusive allegiance to Christ. When put to the test with the growth of emperor worship, it demanded commitment to Christ against Caesar.

From the Roman point of view, the problem lay in the Christian and not in the Roman attitude. Christians, not Romans, were intolerant. Rome did not officially and systematically persecute Christians until about 250 C.E. Before that time, persecutions were local and spasmodic. The first, 64–68 C.E., represented the half-mad Emperor Nero's effort to find a scapegoat after he set fire to Rome in a grandiose scheme of urban renewal. The second, 91–96 C.E., was restricted largely to Asia Minor and involved more local harassment than official persecution. In the third, in which Christians began to suffer persecution on account of the name, the emperor Trajan advised the governor of Bithynia, Pliny, to avoid careless accusations and to punish only those who remained obstinate. Pliny showed a certain objectivity in reporting that charges of immorality were false. In the fourth, the emperor Hadrian also exercised commendable restraint. In the fifth, the emperor Marcus Aurelius persecuted Christians somewhat more severely, but he objected chiefly to their obstinacy. In the sixth, about 200 to 202 C.E., persecution struck heaviest in Alexandria and Carthage, but the terms were still the same.

The first real blow came under the emperor Decius, about 250 C.E. Belatedly the emperor began to recognize what a powerful counterforce Christianity represented. It had become "an empire within the empire." Even here, the emperor proceeded in appropriate legal fashion. He first issued a law requiring every citizen to offer a sacrifice on a stated day. Everyone had to obtain a certificate to that effect. Only when one refused would he or she suffer imprisonment and, as a last resort, death. After Decius, Christians experienced only three more periods of severe persecution — under Gallus II (251–52), Valerian (275–60), and Diocletian (303–11). The last was the worst, a last-gasp effort to stop Christianity once and for all. By that time, however, Christianity was too strong. Constantine doubtless saw that further attempts at suppression were futile when he decided to cast his lot with the church.

Much in the preceding data points to Roman tolerance. Rome made room for other religions or beliefs, and it proceeded reluctantly in the suppression of Christianity. Why, then, did it choose to persecute at all?

The answer to this question is complex. Required, first, is a distinction between popular opposition and harassment and official suppression. Popular opposition stemmed from several sources: (1) misunderstanding of the nature of Christian observances, (2) Christian aloofness, (3) strangeness of Christian doctrines, for example, the doctrine of the resurrection, (4) suspicion of immoral behavior among Christians, and (5) belief that Christians were the cause of calamities befalling Rome because of their refusal to worship the gods.

Official opposition was related to these, but it focused more directly on the charge of treason. Within the Roman Empire such a charge had an increasingly religious cast as the state religion centered in the worship of the emperor. To refuse to pay homage to the emperor and the gods by offering the public sacrifices, however perfunctory they might have seemed, was treasonable. It could bring calamity upon the state; for, in the Roman mind, the state's welfare depended on doing the prescribed rituals. The devout masses regularly blamed Christian refusal to do these things as the cause of natural disasters, military defeats, or barbarian victories. "When the Tiber rises as high as the city walls,... " Tertullian lamented, "the cry is, 'Away with Christians to the lions!' "[1]

From the Roman point of view, the problem was Christian exclusivism to the point of obstinacy. "What could be wrong," they wanted to know, "with going through the perfunctory ceremony the law required? What harm could there be even in paying homage to subordinate deities, even if one believed in a Supreme Deity?" To put the issue in modern terms, offering the votive offering would be like saying the pledge of allegiance to the American flag.

While recognizing the perfunctory character of the rites, Christians still refused to do them. Why? Because they understood the observances to be inseparably connected, as they indeed were, with the worship of many gods and lords, even of the emperor himself. And they worshiped but one Lord and God. God tolerated no others.

It may seem strange that the Romans did not force the Jews to do the same things, but they had a perfect rationale. The Jews were not Roman citizens. The fate of the empire, therefore, did not hinge on their devotion to the gods of Rome. By and large, Christians were Roman citizens, and the fate of the empire did depend on their devotion. To the average Roman, therefore, it was unthinkable that Romans could desert their ancestral gods to worship the God of the Jews. To do so was treasonable not only because the emperor was part of the pantheon but also because the welfare of the empire depended on devotion to the gods who had made Rome great.

What inspired the Roman intolerance was the success of the Christian mission. The Jews, too, would have felt the lash of persecution had they converted masses of Gentiles. They did convert many but not enough to alarm the Romans. Requirements like circumcision inhibited conversions. Christianity, however, did convert masses of Gentiles. The more it succeeded in this, the more intense became the persecution. The Romans could tolerate Christianity, but they could not grant freedom to propagate the faith that Christianity required. Such freedom undermined the absolute loyalty Rome expected of its citizens — loyalty to the emperor and loyalty to the gods who had made Rome great.

Rome could never have given birth to religious liberty — tolerance, yes; religious liberty, no. Polytheism could not go beyond tolerance.

The Grandparent of Religious Liberty

Religious liberty is a child of the monotheism of Christianity. This being so, Jewish monotheism is its grandparent. The Jewish people might have given birth to religious liberty had they drawn out fully the implications of their belief in one God. Some Old Testament writers came close. The Exile helped them to see that God did not confine God's self to Palestine or even to the Jewish people. The author of Isaiah 40–55 expressed this discovery when he named Cyrus, the Medo-Persian king, the Lord's "anointed" (Isa. 45:1) and said that God was raising up a servant "for a light to the Gentiles" (42:6, 49:6), that he might "be my salvation unto the end of the earth" (49:6). The author of Jonah reflected a comparable universalism when he presented Jonah as a missionary sent by God for the salvation of the Ninevites.

Such views did not prevail in later Jewish thinking. The return from the Exile and reconstruction of the Temple in Jerusalem once more gave new life to the idea of a territorial and national limitation of God. God was Israel's God. One day God would vindicate Israel against all other nations. This narrow conception reached a new level during the Maccabean era. In the second century B.C.E. the Maccabees countered the Hellenization of Judaism with a heightened nationalism. Their God would allow no accommodation to Greek customs.

About the same time, a group known as the Essenes arose. They regarded all Jews except themselves as virtual apostates and taught love for "fellow covenanters," that is, Essenes, but hatred of "the foreigner." Their writings, many of which were found in the Dead Sea area in 1947, are filled with particularism. God was their God. One day God would send angels to crush the hated enemies of this true covenant community.

In the time of Jesus there were also "Zealots," Jewish nationalists committed to the expulsion of the Romans and the independence of the Jewish nation. Some scholars have seen a connection between Zealots and Essenes, but this is uncertain. The Essenes did join others in the Jewish War in 68 C.E., only to be wiped out by the Romans.

Judaism of the early Christian era did have sects that manifested greater tolerance than the Maccabees, Essenes, or Zealots.

The Sadducees, the aristocratic priestly ruling class, were tolerant of varied opinions within Judaism so long as these did not threaten the Temple worship. The Pharisees, a respected sect whose interest focused chiefly on the study of the Torah, likewise, gave much latitude as long as certain views or customs did not undermine the Law, God's revealed will. The Pharisaic sect was noted for its legal disputations. From before the Christian era a liberal party, followers of Rabbi Hillel, and a conservative party, followers of Rabbi Shammai, continually handed down differing judgments about the rules of behavior. Many of the varied opinions were codified during the early third century in the Mishnah.

There was enough tolerance that some Sadducees and Pharisees could admire Jesus' teaching, and a few become his followers. Even the broadest tolerance of these two sects, however, reached its extremity when the early Christian mission threatened the twin pillars of first-century Judaism. The Christian threat to Temple and Law prompted Jewish persecution of Christianity. The charge that the religious leaders, evidently Sadducees and Pharisees combined, laid down against Stephen was "speaking blasphemous words against Moses and God," which translated into "saying that Jesus, this Nazarean, will destroy this place [the Temple] and change the customs which Moses delivered to us" (Acts 6:11, 14, author's translation).

Not all Jews agreed that persecution was an answer to the threat. Gamaliel II made an eloquent plea for tolerance when the Jerusalem Sanhedrin was about to suppress the preaching of the early apostles. His answer came close to the true foundation of religious liberty. He observed that similar movements, revolts led by a certain Theudas and by Judas the Galilean, had come to naught. Thus, he counseled, it would be better to leave Peter and the others alone, "for if this plan or this deed is merely human, it will perish, but if it is from God, you will not be able to destroy it — lest you be found opponents of God" (Acts 5:38–39, author's translation). Gamaliel's reasoning falls short of the real basis for religious liberty in that it addressed itself only to an intra-Jewish sect. Nevertheless, it pointed in the right direction. Gamaliel was willing to let God decide. One can neither examine the conscience of one's fellows nor foresee how movements or views will fit into God's long-range plan. Better to allow error than to oppose God.

The Sanhedrin followed Gamaliel's counsel (Acts 5:39). Unhappily, however, another approach soon won out. Its chief advocate was Gamaliel's pupil, Saul of Tarsus, the eventual leader of the mission he tried to suppress. Saul, a self-confessed Zealot "of my ancestral traditions" (Gal. 1:14, NASB),[2] felt in an exaggerated way the threat Christianity posed to both Temple and Law. By both Luke's (Acts 8:3; 9:21) and his own account (Gal. 1:13, 23), he sought to destroy the new movement. His attitude may not have been typical, but it received the sanction of the Jewish authorities. Moreover, after Paul's conversion others within Judaism, or conservative Jewish Christianity, continued the efforts at suppression. Christians long complained that Jews in various local areas incited persecution through public officials.

Judaism failed to implement the implications of monotheism for religious liberty. Jewish monotheism could not tolerate the aggressive missionary force of early Christianity any more than Roman polytheism could. Monotheism had to become truly universal. However close some may have come to the discovery, none realized with the force and clarity of Jesus that God extends God's love equally to *all* persons, irrespective of race, nation, creed, or even behavior. Judaism knew the command, "Love your neighbor as yourself" (Lev. 19:18, RSV). Until Jesus reinterpreted it, however, most Jews understood "neighbor" to mean "fellow Jew." Despite restricting his mission during his lifetime to his own people, Jesus interpreted it to mean "any human being." It was evidently the Qumran Essenes he had specially in mind when he quoted some as teaching, "You shall love your neighbor and hate your enemy" (Matt. 5:43, NRSV), but the saying doubtless summarized a widely held feeling. Against it he demanded love of enemies "because God causes the sun to shine over evil and good persons and the rain to fall on righteous and unrighteous persons" (Matt. 5:45, author's translation). It was this understanding of monotheism that eventually helped give birth to religious liberty.

The Stillbirth of Religious Liberty

Religious liberty was in travail a long time. For centuries Christians practiced the worst kind of intolerance. Many have placed the blame for intolerance on Christianity, and especially monotheism.

Added to Christian monotheism and missionary zeal was another factor of intolerance: the elevation of Christianity as the official state religion. This, and not monotheism, established intolerance as a public virtue, and it originated in Rome rather than in Jerusalem.

As regards intolerance, Christianity conceded nothing to its competitors, whether the state religion, the oriental cults, or the philosophies. All were seen as at best poor specimens of religion and at worst totally perverse. Christianity demanded absolute allegiance to the one true God revealed in Jesus Christ. Nothing, not even the state, could expect a commitment that transcended that allegiance.

The crucial issue is whether the exclusive demand that Christianity laid on its adherents was a necessary cause of intolerance. This writer would contend that the reverse is probably the case. To make this kind of demand, Christianity had to have freedom, complete freedom. More than tolerance was at stake here. Tolerance would have been enough had Christianity been content to be one faith among many. But it was not content with that. It had to be *the* faith. To be *the* faith, it had to have complete freedom to demand absolute allegiance, to propagate itself as *the* faith. The test of whether Christianity wanted religious liberty, therefore, would not reside in its claims but in whether it would demand the same right for its competitors. In brief, it would have to ask that they too could claim absolute allegiance.

The famous Edict of Milan, issued by Constantine and Licinius in 313 C.E., shows the freedom for all religions was exactly what Christians had been pleading for. The edict guaranteed individual freedom of conscience, granted Christianity full rights on an equality with other recognized religions, and restored confiscated church property. The central provision decreed "that it was proper that we should give to Christians, as well as to all others, the right to follow that religion which to each of them appeared best."[3]

Religious liberty had been born! Unfortunately, it did not live long. That its expiration was not due to Christian monotheism and missionary zeal alone will be demonstrated in the next chapter. At the moment it suffices to point out that Christians before Constantine had not asked for an establishment of Christianity. It was understandable that some would welcome a special privilege after years of persecution, but none sought or expected it. What prompted the establishment of Christianity was the ancient Roman conviction that the welfare of the state depended on religion. It was Constantine and his successors who, from this perspective, concluded that the empire would fare best if Christianity alone were the state religion. By the time of Theodosius, religious intolerance had become a public virtue.

Christian monotheism and the resultant Christian mission did not necessitate intolerance. They generated intolerance only when mixed with the theory that the welfare of the state depended on a single type of religious devotion. This point can be sustained further by looking at what Christians actually sought before the Edict of Milan. Did they demand liberty for themselves alone? Or did they see it as a universal right?

Liberty as a universal right clearly represents their view. In the mid-second century Justin Martyr entered an eloquent plea for the freedom to believe without constraint. Tertullian of Carthage, writing at the beginning of the third century, echoed the same sentiment in greater detail. Religious liberty, he stated," is a fundamental human right, a privilege of nature, that every person should worship according to his or her own convictions. One person's religion neither helps nor harms another person." He added, "It is not in the nature of religion to coerce religion, which must be adopted freely and not by force."[4]

Lactantius, tutor of Constantine's ill-fated son Crispus, wrote the charter statement for religious liberty. "It is only in religion that liberty has chosen to dwell," he wrote. "For nothing is so much a matter of free will as religion, and no one can be required to worship what one does not will to worship. One can perhaps pretend, but one cannot will."[5]

So far as the writer knows, no Christian before the time of Constantine demanded liberty for Christians alone. Admittedly, some did not extend the implications of their views to heretics. Tertullian, for instance, could write: "Heretics may properly be compelled, not enticed, to duty. Obstinacy must be corrected, not coaxed."[6] Further, it has to be conceded that, before Constantine, Christians were not in a position to ask for special favors. Yet the question remains: Did they really aspire to a privileged status because of the impetus of the missionary drive issuing from monotheism? The evidence for that is negative. Even when privileges were given, some Christians did not forget that religious liberty is a universal right.

Religious liberty was born in this era, but it was stillborn. The church entered a long period of travail before it could again be born, this time successfully.

For Further Reading

Bates, M. Searle. *Religious Liberty: An Inquiry.* New York: Harper and Brothers, 1945, pp. 132–39.

The Early Church and the State. Ed. Agnes Cunningham, SSCM. Sources of Early Christian Thought. Philadelphia: Fortress Press, 1982.

Greenslade, S. L. *Church and State from Constantine to Theodosius.* London: SCM Press, 1964.

Ruffini, Francesco. *Religious Liberty.* Trans. J. Parker Heyes. New York: G. P. Putnam's Sons, 1912.

For Review

1. Review in chapter 1 the distinction between toleration and religious liberty.

2. In what ways were the Romans tolerant? To what extent could they be said to have allowed religious liberty?

3. Why did Roman polytheism encourage toleration but not religious liberty?

4. Why did Judaism, although monotheistic, not give birth to religious liberty?

5. To what extent did Judaism tolerate differing views? What limited toleration of Christianity?

6. Discuss the charge that Christian monotheism inspired intolerance.

7. In what way did Christian monotheism and missionary drive give birth to religious liberty as contrasted with toleration?

Notes

1. *Apology*, 40; ANF 3:47.
2. From the *New American Standard Bible* (La Habra, Calif.: Lockman Foundation, 1971); published by Creation House, Inc., Carol Stream, Ill. All succeeding quotations from this version are indicated by the abbreviation NASB in parentheses.
3. Cited in Eusebius, *Ecclesiastical History*, X, v, 4.
4. *Divine Institutes*, 54; PL 6:1061.
5. *Scorpiace*, II, 1; CC 2:1071.
6. Ibid.

Chapter 5

The Long Travail
of Religious Liberty

ALTHOUGH CHRISTIANS witnessed the birth of religious liberty in the Edict of Milan, they soon discovered that it was still-born. Constantine thought that Christianity was the tonic needed for a failing empire and moved promptly toward establishing it as the state religion. The result was forced belief and the suppression of dissent. This decision initiated a long era of travail for religious liberty as the Eastern Roman (Byzantine) Empire, then the barbarians, then the so-called Holy Roman Empire, and finally the new states of Europe imitated the Constantinian pattern.

Christian monotheism and the Christian mission were not the ingredients that activated religious persecution. Christians, however, were accessories after the fact and, for the most part, willing accomplices. Relieved that persecution had come to an end, they readily consented to receive imperial favor, including assistance in converting the empire to Christianity. Religious leaders justified the help that was proffered, even coercion.

Within the long era of travail, there were few signs of religious liberty's survival. Occasional signs did appear, nevertheless, and they prefigured a better day, when religious liberty would be born to live.

A Holy Alliance

Space will not allow a detailed statement about the Holy Alliance. However, the fact that the alliance that Constantine contracted with Christianity, or imposed on it, had so much to do with retarding the birth of religious liberty requires further discussion. Why did Constantine adopt Christianity as the state religion and thus set off the chain of intolerance?

His decision was doubtless related to a genuine conversion experience, tinged with some superstition. From a political standpoint, the emperor almost certainly discerned in Christianity a powerful cohesive force that could unite a fragmented empire and restore it to former glories. After eliminating Licinius he moved by gradual stages from freedom for all religions to preferential treatment of Christianity. A few years after the Edict of Milan, Constantine lifted the tax burden from the clergy and arranged other bonuses. He and his mother, Helena, built and opulently furnished churches all over the empire. In 321 he made Sunday a legal holiday in honor of Christ. Then, frustrated by the obstinacy of pagan religion in Old Rome, in 330 he moved the capital to Byzantium, renamed Constantinople. In the new capital he sought to wipe out every trace of the old religion and to install Christianity as the only faith of the city. Constantine did not force conversions, but he fancied himself as the "thirteenth apostle" and "bishop of those outside the church." The church had found a zealous ally in its missionary task.

It was not in connection with conversion of non-Christians, however, that intolerance and persecution reared their heads. Rather, it was in connection with schisms and heresies that threatened not only the unity of the church but also of the empire. First, there was the Donatist schism in North Africa. At the request of the Donatists themselves, Constantine sent a commission to investigate charges against Caecilian, bishop of Carthage. The Donatists refused to accept the conclusion of the commission and challenged state involvement in their affairs. But the damage had been done. Constantine had already shown his sense of responsibility for the well-being of church as well as empire.

However fateful the commission investigating the Donatist schism, it was of small consequence compared to Constantine's intervention in the Arian dispute. Arianism had a far wider impact geographically than Donatism. All over the eastern part of the empire debates and even riots fractured the peace and harmony that had attracted Constantine to Christianity. The emperor called a universal council of bishops to settle the dispute between Arians and Orthodox over the nature of Christ. Although Constantine did not directly determine the outcome, once the bishops decided against Arius and his followers, he proceeded to enforce the decision by sending Arius and obstinate Arians into exile. From that time on emperors, and later, kings, intervened at will to enforce conformity to ecclesiastical norms.

Constantine had set a pattern of involvement in church matters that was to have continuing significance for religious liberty. In the East, where the Roman Empire survived until 1453 with Byzantium (Constantinople) as its capital, emperors enforced decrees of church councils with great rigor. They deposed, imprisoned, and exiled heretics and dissidents. The result was fragmentation of Eastern Christians into dozens of separate sects. In the West, Charlemagne emulated Constantine both in aiding the Christian mission and in keeping a hand in church affairs. When he concluded his conquest of the Saxons, he decreed the death penalty for participation in pagan sacrifices and for evading baptism. He convened councils and directed theologians to deal with heresies and enforced decisions against heretics.

The end products of these developments were the crusades against unbelievers and heretics and the Inquisition. The crusades were the means employed by the secular powers, with the consent and encouragement of the church, to convert the infidel and to reform the heretic and schismatic. They were organized at first to assist the eastern Roman Empire in repelling the Turkish invaders. The first crusade began in 1095. The growth of schisms and heresies in the West between 1000 and 1400 C.E., however, led to the use of crusades to suppress dissent at home. The continuing rationale was that of Constantine: a wholesome state depends on fidelity of all its citizens to the same religion. In the end the crusade proved to be the most effective solution for the elimination of the medieval Cathari, a heretical sect that, about 1200 C.E., numbered in the millions in southern France and northern Italy.

While the secular powers were using the military arm to compel belief, the church was employed in Inquisition. The Inquisition was not a device used by civil authorities, but it would never have succeeded without the Holy Alliance. After the establishment of Christianity as the official religion of the empire, bishops frequently enlisted the aid of civil officials in enforcing discipline within their dioceses. As dissent increased in the Middle Ages, bishops began to organize opposition in church councils. A local council meeting at Rheims in 1157 made provision for branding and banishing heretics and hinted at the death penalty. In 1179 the Third Lateran Council, meeting in Rome, laid the foundation for the organization of a general office of inquisition. It urged the use of civil force and a crusade against heresy.

The powerful Pope Innocent III (1198–1216) called for a crusade against the Cathari of southern France. This crusade enlisted specially trained agents and inquisitors in a rigorous effort to wipe out the Cathari. In 1231 Pope Gregory IX ordered that all heretics should be relinquished to civil authorities for "such punishment as they deserve." A year or so later, he addressed a bull to the duke of Brabant, urging him and other civil authorities to promote the searching out of heresy and to give "counsel, aid, and favor" to the Dominican inquisitors. The Dominicans and Franciscans, two recently formed orders, were authorized specifically to conduct the Inquisition.

Finally, in May 1252, Pope Innocent IV, in the famous bull *Ad extirpanda*, directed to the rulers of Italy, created the final machinery of Inquisition. This document called for full involvement of civil authorities, commended the use of torture, and invoked the severest punishments.

The Inquisition was, in the strictest sense, chiefly a process of investigation for the crime of heresy. Physical coercion was not its chief component, but force figured prominently in the handling of obstinate heretics. Inquisitors relied heavily on informers, and the Inquisition, as H. C. Lea remarked, "rendered every individual as agent of the Inquisition, bound under fearful penalties spiritual and temporal."[1] The burden of proof rested not on the inquisitor but on the accused. Various tortures could be applied when all else failed, so long as the inquisitor had grounds for suspicion. Punishments ranged from imprisonment and confiscation of property to burning.

The Accomplices

In the Inquisition and the crusades, soul liberty suffered its greatest travail. The remarkable thing is that those who, when despised and persecuted, pleaded so eloquently for true liberty became now the accomplices and advocates of persecution. This shift has prompted many persons to single out Christian monotheism and missionary endeavor as the immediate culprits. Although acknowledging that both of these played a part, this writer sees them as accomplices after the fact. They were used in a perverse way to rationalize the coercion employed in maintaining a church state.

Some of the roots of this rationalization antedated the Constantinian era. Tertullian, for example, refused to concede heretics the liberty he demanded for all other persons. Fifty years later, Cyprian of Carthage militantly excluded schismatics and heretics from salvation as well as from fellowship with himself. His reasoning was, "One can no longer have God for his father, who has not the church for his mother," and "Outside the church there is no salvation."[2] As ominous as such threats were, they involved no physical coercion. Schismatics and heretics had the same right to exist as Catholics, and no Christian contemplated seriously the restriction of another's liberty, except within the fellowship of the church. The danger, nevertheless, lay near the surface. And the Holy Alliance uncovered it in due time.

The first Christian justifications of coercion in religious matters came nearly a century after the Edict of Milan. Only one of these, by Optatus, bishop of Milevis, advocated the death penalty. Not all Christians, moreover, agreed that any force should be employed. The eminence of the advocates of coercion, however, especially of Augustine, assured the triumph of intolerance over religious liberty.

It was Augustine's justification that the Middle Ages constantly cited. One must not forget, however, this his mentor and baptizer, Ambrose, bishop of Milan, anticipated him at many points. Ambrose, one-time governor of Roman provinces, clearly espoused the Roman theory that the welfare of the state depended on the devotion of her citizens, especially the emperor, to the appropriate faith. As a Christian, Ambrose believed that this faith was Christianity. As pastor of the emperors when they resided in Milan, he continually worried about the correctness of their beliefs. Although he advocated a quasi-separation of church and state, he fully condoned and encouraged imperial favoritism to Christianity and the Christian mission. He rebuked the emperor Theodosius when the latter forced the Christian citizens of Callinicum, a town on the Euphrates, to make reparations for a Jewish synagogue they had destroyed during a rage against "unbelievers." The order was a sacrilege. He continually urged imperial action against heretics. On grounds that it was his to grant, he refused the plea of the empress Justina, an Arian, for one church building in which she could exercise her faith. Here Ambrose favored church-state separation. "Palaces belong to the emperor, churches to the bishop."[3]

For practical reasons, Augustine was to manifest less concern for the separation of church and state than Ambrose did. North Africa was troubled less by Arianism than Italy. Augustine fully expected the public officials to wipe out the last traces of paganism. Several times he politely declined to intercede with the governor of Africa or local magistrates on behalf of pagans. The official suppression of paganism might appear severe for the moment, he replied, but it would turn out beneficially in the long run.

The implications of this attitude for religious liberty are self-evident. However, this could not match the impact of his argument for the correction of the Donatists. In the early years as a Christian, Augustine sided with those who defended the voluntary nature of religion and opposed the use of force. Thus he, who had once belonged to the heretical Manichaean sect, recalled how he opposed proponents of force against the Manichees. "I can on no account rage against you," he said, "for I must bear with you now as formerly I had to bear with myself, and I must be patient towards you as my associates were with me, when I went madly and blindly astray in your beliefs."[4]

At first, even the Donatist crisis did not evoke a change. Augustine advocated preaching, debate, and pastoral concern as the means of reconciliation. In time, however, he lost patience, partly because the Donatists were a violent sect and partly because he found that force obtained results. In a letter addressed to a Donatist bishop, Augustine contended that although coercion did not produce a conversion, it could create the conditions for genuine conversion. After quoting Proverbs 27:6, he said that it was "better to love with severity than to deceive with leniency."[5] Next, he quoted Luke 14:23 and alluded to the "forceful" conversion of the apostle Paul by Christ. He admitted that the advocacy of coercion in religion represented a change of mind. "But this opinion of mine was overcome not by words of those who convey it, but by the conclusive instances to which they would point."[6]

In summary, force worked. What was important was not the use of force but its objective. In this case the objective was wholly commendable. It held the same benefits as imperial edicts against pagans, that is, conversion to Christianity. In a letter addressed to imperial officer Boniface of North Africa, in 417, Augustine reviewed many of the same points. He refused to concede the Donatist claim that persecution proved that they were the true church. He differentiated between just and unjust persecution. The church's persecution was just because done out of love, for correction, and for restoration.[7]

Other eminent churchmen seconded Augustine. Even John Chrysostom, an otherwise tolerant and pastoral bishop, was willing to accept the use of force at appropriate times and under certain conditions. Generally speaking, however, Christians accepted the assistance of the secular authorities but opposed the death penalty. Room had to be kept for repentance. As Jerome put it, "He who finds himself today led astray by an ungodly belief may come to his senses tomorrow and begin to defend the truth."[8]

From both Ambrose and Augustine the church of the Middle Ages borrowed and refined perspectives that were instrumental in withholding religious liberty. From Ambrose it borrowed the idea of the independency and superiority of the spiritual realm. In the mid-eighth century appeared the famous Donation of Constantine. Purporting to be a bequest of Constantine to Pope Sylvester I out of gratitude for being cured of leprosy, it granted not only rule over the churches in the West but also rule over the temporal order. In effect, the Donation envisioned the pope as Constantine's successor in the West. The emergence of the Frankish Kingdom, then the Holy Roman Empire, and then other national states put this theory to the test again and again. Churchmen, nevertheless, continued to assert it, demanding acquiescence and assistance in the church's designs.

In 1302 the theory reached its ultimate expression in the two swords doctrine of Pope Boniface VIII's famous bull *Unam Sanctum*.

As stated by Boniface, both swords are in the church's control; the temporal sword was to be used *for* the church, the spiritual sword *by* the church. Everything in heaven and on earth falls under the papal dominion, for "it is altogether necessary to salvation for every human creature to be subject to the Roman pontiff." Even for Boniface, this was a hollow claim, but it supplied a powerful base for invoking secular authority in the enforcement of ecclesiastical decrees. All too often in the Middle Ages it was heeded by secular powers.

From Augustine the church of the Middle Ages borrowed a rationale for the Inquisition. Other leaders also justified the use of force. It remained for Thomas Aquinas, however, to put together the final brief.

Aquinas stated the principle that neither God nor the church desires the death of the sinner, whether heretical or not. The aim is the sinner's conversion, restoration, and reconciliation with the church (2 Tim. 2:24–26). Death removes the possibility of repentance. Only stubborn heretics come under the biblical instruction to reject them after two or three warnings. Such should be not only restrained but "compelled to come in" if possible (Luke 14:23). Heresy is far more serious than not having believed. It is a crime more serious than destruction of property or murder. Thus the unbeliever should be "compelled" to believe, but heretics who remained steadfast in their heresy and for whom there was no hope of their conversion should be excommunicated and handed over to the secular power to be exterminated "from the world by death."[9]

With this statement religious liberty surely reached its lowest ebb. The conclusion of James Mackinnon that it "cannot be said to have existed at all in the Middle Ages"[10] is not far from the mark. In a few minds, however, a tiny spark of the older Christian view remained. In all fairness, it deserves a word of comment.

Other Voices

The most ardent defenders and exponents of religious liberty have always been the oppressed and persecuted. Although the centuries have produced no great treatises on religious liberty, the Donatists, Arians, Cathari, and many others voiced their pleas. Even within the Catholic Church, it was those who felt the lash of persecution who developed the most enlightened perspectives.

In the decades after Constantine's death in 337, Catholic Christians, as well as Donatists and Arians, began to wish they had looked the gift horse in the mouth. Even before Constantine died, he had begun to relax strictures against Arians, allowing even Arius to return from exile. Constantine himself was baptized on his deathbed by the Arian leader Eusebius of Nicomedia. Then Constantine's son Constantius, who ruled the East, openly espoused Arianism. He wanted, as Constantine did, one faith for the whole empire. In this case, he chose the Arian form.

Constantius's harassment and persecution of Catholic leaders provoked outcries and pleas for separation of church and sate. Hilary, bishop of Poitiers, France, contested the use of political authority in matters of faith. Ambrose took a similar stance when ordered to transfer the cathedral of Milan to the empress Justina for Arian use. Ambrose wrote the emperor Valentinian II that neither could he hand it over nor could the emperor receive it. The emperor should not imagine that he owns all things, as he claimed. If he wished a long reign, he should be subject to God. Palaces were his, but not churches.[11]

The most enlightened statement came from the pen of John Chrysostom during his younger years as a priest in Antioch. In his treatise *On the Priesthood* he represented a pastoral outlook: "For Christians above all persons are not permitted forcibly to correct the failings of those who sin."[12] Although in later writings he consented to the use of force, in this treatise he argued that a physician's handling of the patient depends in part on the latter's will. The patient, therefore, must be willingly in a proper frame of mind by persuasion, perseverance, and patience, "for he cannot be dragged back by force, nor constrained by fear, but must be led back by persuasion to the truth from which he originally swerved."[13]

Medieval Christianity had a short memory about religious liberty. Its virtually complete triumph, the establishment of Christendom, eliminated the minority consciousness of oppression that Christians had experienced earlier. Minority groups always have a sensitivity to freedom that the majority does not have. The persecuted know the reality of persecution.

The seed of liberty is so tough, however, that it managed to survive even the Middle Ages. The parable of the tares so gripped the minds of some that they would not explain it away. As much as Bernard of Clairvaux contributed to the suppression of heresy, he sounded welcome notes of contrast to Thomas Aquinas. He would capture heretics "not with arms but with arguments." He would use force only when they threatened to lead others into error. Force would benefit society; it would not convert the error-stricken. Bernard said: "We approve zeal, but do not urge the actuality, for faith must be urged, not imposed."[14]

Francis of Assisi left no statements on religious liberty, but he exemplified another way of winning believers. In a time when military crusades were the chief means, he went among the Saracens as a humble follower of Jesus. He was not successful, but, in the long run, neither were the crusaders. Ironically, the church chose to make the Franciscan order an arm of the Inquisition. The Franciscan missionary to the Moslems, Ramon Lull, went a long way toward the development of a Christian apologetic based on the force of love and logic rather than the force of arms. His writings presented Moslem, Jewish, Greek Christian, Roman Christian, and Tatar views with remarkable tolerance, fairness, and kindliness. While on a missionary excursion in North Africa in 1315, Lull was stoned to death by a Moslem mob.

The stories of Bernard, Francis, and Ramon Lull epitomize the contradictions that filled these long centuries of travail for religious liberty. The fertilized seed was there, but could not come to term. The birth pangs were not yet intensified by enough dissent and persecution to bring it forth. They were growing more intense, however, and within a century or two religious liberty would be born.

For Further Reading

Bainton, Roland H. *The Travail of Religious Liberty*. Philadelphia: Westminster Press, 1951.

Bates, M. Searle. *Religious Liberty: An Inquiry*. New York: Harper and Brothers, 1945, pp. 132–48.

Greenslade, S. L. *Church and State from Constantine to Theodosius*. London: SCM Press, 1964.

Peters, Edward., ed. *Heresy and Authority in Medieval Europe*. Philadelphia: University of Pennsylvania Press, 1980.

Tierney, Brian. *The Crisis of Church and State, 1050–1300*. Englewood Cliffs, N.J.: Prentice-Hall, 1964.

For Review

1. Discuss the reasons for Constantine's favoritism toward Christianity. Is any of this thinking present in America today? Where?

2. Discuss the consequences of the Holy Alliance for religious liberty.

3. Review the discussion of the development of the Inquisition. What factors encouraged its development?

4. Review the reasoning of Christians in support of coercion. Evaluate the reasoning that force worked. Do you hear such reasoning today?

5. What safeguards might have prevented the religious oppression of the Middle Ages?

Notes

1. *History of the Inquisition in Spain*, 4 vols. (New York: Macmillan Co., 1906–7), 4:91.

2. *On the Unity of Catholic Church*, 6; ANF 5:423.

3. *Letter* 20, 19; LCC 5:214.

4. *Against the Letter of a Manichee*, 3; NPNF 4:130; PL 42:174–75.

5. *Letter*, 93, 4; PL 33:323; NPNF 1:383.

6. Ibid., 93, 17; NPNF 1:388.

7. *Letter*, 185, 24.

8. *Commentary on the Gospel of Matthew*, II, 13; PL 26:93

9. *Summa Theologica*, part II, section ii, question 11, article 304.

10. *A History of Modern Liberty*, 4 vols. (London: Longmans, Green, 1906–41), 1:x.

11. *Letter*, 20, 19.

12. *On the Priesthood*, II, 3; NPNF 9:41; PG 48:634.

13. *On the Priesthood*, II, 4; NPNF 9:41.

14. *Sermon on the Song of Songs*; PL 183:1086, 1101.

Chapter 6

Final Birth Pangs

THE FINAL PANGS that gave birth to religious liberty came during the sixteenth and seventeenth centuries. It is a curious fact of history that Protestantism did not give birth to religious liberty during the Reformation. The Protestant principle that no human institution can have the final say favored the birth of liberty. Moreover, Protestants, along with other Christians, were sickened by a century or more of crusades, inquisitions, and repression. They waited expectantly for the birth of the child.

The Reformation began with the promise of liberty. Early in his struggles with Roman officialdom, Luther strongly sustained complete liberty for all persons. Political realities, however, burst the bubble. Almost without exception, the major reformers came not only to accept but to give a rationale for suppression of heretics. Whatever may have been their ideal, in practice they scarcely bettered their own oppressors in the Roman Church. Nearly every nation in Europe trembled with violence and persecution for a century and a half. The so-called Enlightenment of the last half of the seventeenth century represented a general outcry for an end to bloodshed and coercion in religion.

However dark the scene, the sufferings of these centuries were labor pains that would force the child from the womb. As in the early centuries of Christian history, the persecuted and harassed Protestants of the left-wing Reformation and humanist sympathizers uttered the most eloquent pleas for liberty. In the new American colonies first, then eventually in the states of Europe, their pleas were heard. The time of begetting was near.

Religious Liberty's Pains

Before hearing some of the voices that pleaded for it, it will be helpful to examine the pains that in time helped to give birth to religious liberty.

Religious Wars

Religious wars wracked Europe and England for over a century. At the outset of the Reformation the leaders of the Holy Roman Empire (Germany), already divided politically, lined up on both sides of the controversy. Both Catholic and Protestant princes formed leagues for mutual defense about 1522. The balance of power was close enough that neither could win a clear majority in the German Diet. Consequently, Protestants managed to wrangle some concessions. The withdrawal of these privileges led to numerous skirmishes.

The so-called Peace of Augsburg in 1555 produced an uneasy settlement that followed the principle that the religion of a ruler would determine the religion of that ruler's territory. The replacement of one ruler by another, however, frequently meant a change of religion in a territory. The option of inhabitants was either to be converted or move.

The outcome was the bitter Thirty Years' War, which engaged most of Europe between 1618 and 1648. By the time of its consummation Europeans were sickened of religion as well as war. The Peace of Westphalia recognized Calvinists as well as Lutherans as Protestants and gave both Protestants and Catholics some liberty of worship. True liberty, however, was a long way off in Europe.

Switzerland, divided among its independent cantons between Catholic and Protestant forces, suffered more briefly in two wars. As in Germany, Swiss Catholics and Protestants formed leagues. The wars, in 1529 and in 1531, resulted in another territorial arrangement, some cities and cantons remaining Catholic, others going Protestant. The Zurich reform leader, Huldreich Zwingli, fought and died in the second war. Subsequently, Switzerland suffered little open fighting.

Strongly Catholic France experienced bitter spasmodic fighting for more than thirty years. The first of eight religious wars began in 1562. Although Catholics outnumbered Protestants almost ten to one, the wars proved inconclusive. They showed little more than that Catholics could not destroy Protestantism, and that Protestantism could not supplant Catholicism as the religion of the nation. From these conflicts, however, emerged a disdain of both Protestant and Catholic passions among many French people and the tolerant attitude reflected in the Edict of Nantes in 1598.

The Netherlands, too, suffered birth pangs from religious wars. In this case it was Catholic Spain, whose king was also ruler of the Netherlands, that caused the grief. In 1566 Philip II, an ardent Catholic, sought to impose the decisions of the Catholic Council of Trent on the Netherlands. Combined with burdensome taxes, this act produced a revolt. The wars resulted in the division of the Netherlands — the north, Holland, becoming Protestant; the south, remaining Catholic.

England, because the Reformation progressed slowly and haltingly, was fortunate to have a delay in religious conflict. It erupted finally in the seventeenth century when Puritans, who felt that the reform was not thorough enough, revolted. Calvinists in theology, they sought reform along Calvinist lines. The English Civil War lasted from about 1637 to 1646. After a period of nonmonarchical government, the English people recalled their monarch, Charles II. The desire of Charles and his brother James for the restoration of Roman Catholicism led to James's exile. The new monarchs, William and Mary of Orange, represented the general sentiment of the English people when they issued the Toleration Act of 1689. By this document all but Roman Catholics and anti-Trinitarians received the right to public worship according to the dictates of conscience.

Persecution

Religious wars affected other countries but less significantly. Besides the wars, another source of pain was persecution. Both

Catholics and Protestants persecuted. The chief victims were the radical reformers, minority groups that disturbed both Catholic and Protestant establishments.

Luther did not start out as a persecutor. Until the Peasants' War, 1523–25, he espoused a broad policy of religious toleration. His principle, stated at Worms before the German Diet, was: "The conscience must not be bound by anything except but the Word of God." After the peasants' revolt, however, Luther began to change. He emphasized then the duty of the magistrates and princes to keep order. This would include the suppression of public heresy, though Luther defended the right of private conscience. By 1530 Luther and his followers accepted the death penalty for radicals. In 1535 both Catholic and Protestant armies gathered to wipe out mercilessly the Anabaptists at Munster.

The reformers of Zurich and Geneva, notably Zwingli and Calvin, manifested less tolerance than Luther. In Zurich, Zwingli became the first Protestant persecutor. Although he associated closely with the Anabaptist leaders Conrad Grebel and Felix Manz for several years and held views similar to theirs, he could not tolerate dissent. As in Germany, civil rather than religious authorities applied coercion, but at Zwingli's discretion. Manz was put to death by drowning. Another Anabaptist leader, George Blaurock, was horribly tortured and martyred. By 1535 hardly an Anabaptist remained in Switzerland.

In Geneva, Calvin showed an intolerance to nonconformists not surpassed by that of Roman Catholic inquisitors. Although Geneva became a haven for harassed Protestants, it also expelled many others who did not agree with Calvin's views on predestination, the Trinity, the sacraments, or other matters. The most celebrated case involved a brilliant Spanish heretic named Michael Servetus. He escaped the clutches of Catholic authorities in Vienna and fled to Geneva. No doubt he thought Calvin would offer refuge and possibly accept his views. Instead, Calvin had him arrested and tried before the town council. Calvin himself served as prosecutor. Servetus was burned alive on October 27, 1553.

The awful pain of Michael Servetus could not be forgotten. It was this kind of suffering that would bear the true fruit of religious liberty. In 1903, the 350th anniversary of the burning, Genevans erected a monument as a reminder of an "error" their great forefather John Calvin made in the burning of this man.

Followers of Calvin displayed a like intolerance. In Scotland John Knox assured the complete triumph of Calvinism and the elimination of all traces of Roman Catholicism. In the Netherlands Protestants displayed a measure of tolerance as they opened a door to Anabaptist (Mennonite) refugees in the awful years after Munster. In the seventeenth century, however, strict Calvinists refused the same tolerance to Arminians, removing them from office and persecuting them vigorously for a time. But this intolerance soon faded. After 1632 Europeans regarded the Netherlands as a model of religious tolerance.

English Protestant reformers perhaps manifested the largest measure of tolerance. The executions that occurred in Henry VIII's reign were motivated more by political than by religious considerations, even if the charges were sometimes religious. After the rigorous Catholic restoration under "Bloody Mary," 1553–58, the nation was ready for the lenient Protestantism of Elizabeth. Elizabeth instituted what Roland Bainton has called "the way of comprehension." Under this arrangement few suffered on account of theological views. Elizabeth set limits of diversity in respect to worship rather than theology, believing, like Constantine, that right worship guaranteed the well-being of the nation.

Few suffered for nonconformity during Elizabeth's long and wise reign (1558–1603). Insistence on uniformity of worship, however, proved a source of much grief under her less able successors, James I and Charles I. These monarchs turned a deaf ear to Puritan desires for further reform. When more Puritans began to meet in irregular gatherings where they could worship in the manner that suited their views of reform, the monarchs responded with imprisonment, fines, confiscation of property, and other measures. Still, few persons died for nonconformity.

After the Commonwealth era (1649–60), Charles II continued the policy of uniformity. Again dissenters suffered imprisonment and other penalties. The desire of Charles II and James II to reintroduce Catholicism to England, however, caused a lightening of the hand of persecution. In 1672 Charles issued a broad Declaration of Indulgence, which restricted only the most radical dissenters. The nation as a whole, however, was not ready for tolerance, especially of Roman Catholicism. With the support even of Baptists, Quakers, and other minority sects, Parliament restored the policy of conformity by a Test Act of 1675.

The Baptist John Bunyan's story reflects well the travail of dissenters. As a sixteen-year-old youth Bunyan joined other Puritans in Cromwell's "New Model Army" in the struggle against Charles I. During his two years of service in this unusual army, he experienced a kind of conversion. After leaving the army his religious convictions grew. Eventually he joined a Baptist congregation at Bedford and later became its pastor. During Cromwell's reign this posed no problem, for Cromwell favored independents and separatists. When Charles II restored the monarchy in 1660, however, Parliament restored legislation requiring conformity of worship and forbidding unlicensed meetings and preaching. Under one of these acts Bunyan went to prison for refusal to stop preaching without a license. Had he known his rights better, he might have been freed after about three months. As it was, he spent six years in Bedford jail, was released briefly, rearrested, and returned to jail for another six years. He was freed under Charles II's Declaration of Indulgence, then reimprisoned for about six months when Parliament passed the Test Act. He died in 1688, a year before William and Mary issued the Toleration Act that would have protected him against any further harassment on account of his faith.

The intolerance Bunyan suffered was mild compared to that many others knew. Yet even it must not be underestimated or forgotten. When Bunyan went to jail, he left four young children, one a blind daughter, "dearer to me," he said, "than all else I had beside." His wife bore the burden of earning a living and rearing the family. To assist, Bunyan made shoelaces, which his wife peddled. And he wrote. But long confinement sapped his mind and drained his spirit. Bunyan's output in his second period of imprisonment was far below that in the first. The price he paid for the free exercise of his faith can never be counted.

The pain of Bunyan and countless others in England was preparation for a new day. It stirred afresh the embers of sensitivity to suffering and of human perception of that deeper truth of religion that persecution contradicts. Although English Protestants were not yet ready to grant religious liberty to all persons, the Toleration Act of 1689 showed that true liberty would be born soon. The birth pangs had not been in vain.

While Protestants added to the pangs of liberty through persecution, Roman Catholics continued the Inquisition in an effort to recoup their losses to Protestantism. In Spain the Inquisition reached its peak during the reigns of Ferdinand and Isabella under the guidance of Thomas de Torquemada, most ingenious inquisitor of them all. In 1488, about 3,300 persons came before the Inquisition in Toledo. The Jews especially suffered as Spain sought to consolidate the Iberian peninsula as a Christian stronghold.

In France, Francis I launched a vigorous crusade against Protestants after 1533. A number of edicts suppressed publication of Protestant books, ordered the French people to inform on one another, and punished heresy by burning. A special court established to deal with "heresy" (Protestant) cases earned the nickname, "the burning chamber." Francis ordered a massacre of thousands of Waldensians, a medieval sect to which France had given refuge earlier. The change of attitude was doubtless connected with aid and sympathy accorded Protestants by the Waldensians.

Francis's successor, Henry II, continued the reign of terror against Protestants. As in England, however, persecution generated new perceptions. Many of France's elite had Protestant sympathies or actually became Protestant. Concessions to Protestants only inflamed Catholic passions more. The Massacre of St. Bartholomew's Day in 1572 unleashed the flood of Catholic fury. Some contemporary accounts recorded as many as seventy thousand deaths, ten thousand in Paris alone. Rome's persecution of early Christianity produced nothing like that. Here, too, however, a senseless deed prepared for the birth of liberty.

When at last the religious wars ended with the "conversion" of Henry of Navarre, who could become king only by becoming a Catholic, France too experienced tolerance in the Edict of Nantes. This edict, which Henry had promised Protestants if he became king, guaranteed freedom of conscience, allowed Protestants freedom of public assembly in many cities, gave them six councillors in the Parliament, and permitted them to study in the universities. It was not liberty, but it was a start. Reversal of it by the intolerant Louis XIV in 1685 represented a throwback to the Middle Ages. Louis's motto was: "One king, one law, one faith." That strange reversal, which cost France thousands of its finest citizens, helped not only to assure that the French people would seek liberty all the more but also sealed the doom of the French monarchy a century later. From that time forth, *liberté* has been the irrepressible cry of the French.

In England the brief reign of Mary Tudor has been remembered for its brutality in the suppression of Protestantism. The actual number of deaths has often been exaggerated, but Mary's effort to restore Catholicism as the faith of England did cost many lives. The most eminent martyr was Thomas Cranmer, Protestant archbishop of Canterbury under Henry VIII and Edward VI. In ill health and under torture, he signed a recantation of his Protestant views. When led to the stake in Oxford, however, he renounced this act and held the offending hand to the flames to be burned first. His courageous act caught the sympathies of English people everywhere. When Mary died in 1558, the people were fully prepared for the tolerance of Elizabeth I.

In Scotland two martyrdoms did as much as anything to assure the complete triumph of Protestantism. One was the burning of Patrick Hamilton in 1528; the other was the burning of George Wishart in 1546. Among the witnesses to both was "the thundering Scot," John Knox. The first, when he was only thirteen, etched itself indelibly on his mind. The second was still more significant, however, for Knox was a kind of bodyguard to Wishart. Knox himself, captured by the French along with other Wishart followers, spent nineteen months as a galley slave. He did not forget these events when the final contest between Catholicism and Protestantism was waged in Scotland. Unfortunately, his experience braced him against the pull of tolerance that the Reformation should have exerted. As a result, full liberty arrived late in Scotland.

Religious Liberty's Womb

To describe accurately the complex factors that brought forth religious liberty would require a much larger volume than this. The major force was undoubtedly the pains of intolerance and bloodshed. At the same time, however, other, more positive forces were adding to the effect of these.

During the Middle Ages, mystical thought flourished. Mysticism always emphasizes the individual and inward experience. As it does, it undercuts to some degree the force of external authorities, whether church or state.

The Renaissance of the fourteenth century and after carried this process forward in several ways. One was heightening of individual consciousness. Westerners no longer accepted either church or state as final authorities in matters of belief and behavior. They looked within, to the individual conscience. Another was the advance of humanism. Renaissance scholars once again quoted the ancient Greek adage, "Man is the measure of all things." A third was the shift from an otherworldly to a this-worldly outlook. In the Middle Ages the Platonic theory that the spiritual alone is permanent and real, combined with the harshness of life, had encouraged otherworldliness. In the Renaissance, however, people rediscovered nature. They appreciated the physical world as much as people in the Middle Ages had yearned for the other world. They were less willing to surrender their lives to attain the beatific vision. The world was their home, and they wanted to enjoy it as long as possible.

Economic and political considerations also contributed to the development of tolerance, if not religious liberty. The religious wars wreaked such havoc on Europe as to inspire greater tolerance. In the midst of the wars of religion in France, a new political group, calling themselves the *politiques*, arose. They yearned neither for a Catholic nor a Protestant triumph. They wanted peace so that the nation might survive. When revocation of the Edict of Nantes in 1685 produced a flood of Protestant emigrations, the French minister of state issued a memorandum "For the Recall of the Huguenots." He pointed out that, despite controls, France lost eighty thousand to one hundred thousand persons and their capital, including many of the best artisans, organizers, and merchants of France. He challenged the king's authority in the matter: "Kings are indeed masters of the lives and goods of their subjects but never of their opinions, because the inner feelings are beyond their power and because God alone can direct them as He pleases."[1] Even Louis XIV sickened of the repression and remitted penalties from time to time.

In the Netherlands, the Dutch merchant enterprise encouraged tolerance. Despite intolerant attitudes displayed in hyper-Calvinism, the Dutch soon realized that suppression of dissent did irreparable damage to economic and political life. Amsterdam became in the seventeenth century a model of tolerance and haven for the oppressed. Baruch Spinoza, the famous philosopher, described the city as the freest in the world — in publication, in religion, and as a place of refuge. The French and Dutch attitudes had a large impact in England and in the American colonies.

Finally, rationalism contributed to the development of liberty. Rationalism developed alongside acceptance of authority in medieval theology. One of the major questions university teachers debated was the relationship between faith and reason. Scholars such as Peter Abelard (c. 1079–1144) affirmed reason strongly. This strong emphasis flourished also in the Renaissance and left wing of the Protestant Reformation. In the Reformation it was represented particularly by anti-Trinitarians such as Michael Servetus and even by some Anabaptists. However, while rationalism was on the periphery of the Reformation, it became the center of the Enlightenment of the seventeenth century. Combined with individualism, it became a powerful club in the attack on the dogmatism that underlies so much of both Catholic and Protestant intolerance.

Medieval mysticism, the Renaissance, economic and political considerations, and rationalism were important forces in the begetting of religious liberty. It is possible, however, in taking a closer look, to see three groups or movements that contributed more directly still: humanist Christians, the persecuted minorities of Europe, and dissenters in England. The pain bore most heavily upon them.

The Humanists

In the Italian Renaissance humanism began as a cultural phenomenon, involving chiefly a study of Greek and Roman classics. In time, however, it took on a more philosophical character with an accent on the worth of humankind. It was not surprising that humanists became spokespersons for greater tolerance and strong critics of religious oppression.

The most eminent and widely known of the humanists was Erasmus of Rotterdam. Erasmus combined humanism with rationalism and pietism in his doctrine of religious liberty. At the center stood the Christian concept of *agape* love. Love alone, he believed, should prevent inhumanity. The Suffering Servant should be the model. He commanded that we leave the tares alone lest we uproot the wheat. God alone should judge. Erasmus believed that all Christians could agree on essentials and forget about the insignificant. The essentials could be found by study of the Scriptures and the church fathers. For Erasmus, the essentials involved faith in God, the mission of Christ, and proper ethical behavior. Still, Erasmus was practical enough to admit that the severity of his day in dealing with heretics was perhaps necessary. In the end he was willing to bow to the church's authority.

The more humane side of Erasmus, who remained a Roman Catholic, exerted a significant impact on many other humanists, both Catholic and Protestant. Greatest of all apologists for religious liberty among the humanists was Sebastian Castellio. Shortly after the burning of Michael Servetus, Castellio composed his famous treatise *Concerning Heretics*. The book consisted chiefly of a collection of statements of Christian writers from early times to his own day who supported religious liberty, including Luther, Erasmus, Jerome, Augustine, Chrysostom, and John Calvin.

The persecution of heretics, Castellio warned, contemptible as they may be, holds practical dangers: (1) the prince may put to death someone not a heretic; (2) he may punish a heretic more severely than Christian discipline allows. The early Christian fathers, even Augustine, never allowed the death penalty. The fact is, heresy is difficult to define. After investigation, Castellio decided it meant in his day that we regard those as heretics "with whom we disagree."[2] The Scriptures deny such a definition. Instead, they connect heresy with obstinacy of two kinds — obstinacy in regard to behavior and obstinacy in regard to belief. To judge belief is not as simple as to judge behavior. Accordingly, although all may agree that evil persons — murderers or brigands — deserve punishment, not all can agree about punishment of heretics, for they cannot decide what deserves punishment.

Concerning Heretics was not Castellio's first nor last plea for complete liberty. He composed a reply to Calvin's defense of the burning of Michael Servetus. In this treatise Castellio emphasized love as well as uncertainty about doctrine. He pointed out the anomaly of burning persons for doctrine but ignoring scurrility, lying, calumny, avarice, unruly temper, and wrangling. "What can you do with a man who regards scurrility, avarice, and calumny as lighter sins than heresy, card playing, and dancing?" he asked.[3] In reply to Calvin's contention that a strict interpretation of the parable of the tares would destroy the power of magistrates, Castellio distinguished spheres of responsibility. When he puts a robber to death, the magistrate acts against those who have done evil and caused harm. When he puts a heretic to death, he usurps God's prerogative as Judge. He must wait, for he cannot know who is a heretic. How often the persecutors have erred! "Will the Zwinglians and Calvinists alone be free from error?"[4] No, Christians must leave judgment to God. No one can compel others to be good against their will.

Anabaptists and Other Radicals

The brilliant pleas of Castellio met both opposition and acceptance. They had their greatest influence in the Netherlands, where *Concerning Heretics* was twice published in the seventeenth century, and in England. No group of Christians, however, welcomed them more than did the harassed and much maligned Anabaptists.

The Anabaptists framed their own pleas for religious liberty in similar words. Their greatest contribution to liberty lay not in their writings, the remains of which are not extensive, so much as in their practical solution to the problem of state coercion in religion. They favored complete separation of church and state. The principle of church-state separation derived from their belief in the corruption of society and in the necessity of withdrawal from it. The famous Schleitheim Confession, drafted in 1527, radically separated two classes — "good and bad, believing and unbelieving, darkness and light, the world and those who are out of the world, God's temple and idols, Christ and Belial."[5] For the Christian, therefore, the only option is withdrawal from the world and, as a result, misunderstanding, hostility, and persecution by others. In their minds, suffering proved that they were the true church.

The Anabaptists were not the only radicals to express concern for toleration, but they expressed an important voice. David Joris, an eccentric Dutch Anabaptist, argued for religious liberty from an essentially mystical perspective. Faith cannot be outward assent but only an experience of the spirit. Thus defined, neither the church nor the magistrates can set other tests, whether the creeds, the Bible, or the Spirit. Persecution merely identifies the true church, that which follows Christ in suffering persecution. The positive marks of this church are meekness, gentleness, and lowliness, such as Christ himself displayed. Whoever has the most love has the best faith.[6]

Sebastian Franck was the most rationalistic and individualistic of proponents of liberty. The world, he judged, has killed many saints as heretics. It cannot "understand a Christian, much less speak and judge of his way."[7] Franck urged that all persons, Moslems and pagans even, be considered brothers and sisters, as "instructed by God and inwardly drawn by him," even if unbaptized or not having heard the gospel.

English Voices

The plaints of both humanists and Anabaptists were heard and echoed in many parts of Europe during the sixteenth and seventeenth centuries. Among nations favoring Protestantism, England leaned more toward the humanist approach than the others. This was evidenced in Elizabeth's comprehensive approach to reform, which allowed wide latitude in belief even if insisting on conformity in worship. In time, theological latitude opened the way toward a new concept of unity — not unity in the organic sense but unity in denominational diversity. Denominationalism flowered in the seventeenth century. As it did, it made tolerance an even greater practical necessity, for national unity could not survive intolerance.

During the century of agonizing strife, many voices, representing both Anglicans and dissenting groups, cried out for tolerance. Among the earliest strong proponents of complete religious liberty were the Baptists. In 1611 John Smyth's *Confession of Faith* denied the state's jurisdiction in religious affairs. Thomas Helwys wrote *A Short Declaration of the Mistery of Iniquity*, called by W. K. Jordan "the finest and fullest defence which it [religious liberty] had ever received in England" by an Englishman.[8] Helwys pleaded for the freedom of all — Moslems, Jews, and Roman Catholics, as well as Protestants.

In the Commonwealth era Oliver Cromwell and his son Richard sought to maintain full tolerance for all except Roman Catholics, who were seen as a political threat. Agitation by royalists, however, forced him to rule by virtual martial law in favor of Independents. Not surprisingly, Anglicans rather than dissenters wrote the most eloquent pleas for toleration. One noted essay came from Jeremy Taylor, entitled *Discourse of the Liberty of Prophesying*. Because heresy is so hard to define, he contended, no one should be persecuted purely on an article of faith. The civil authorities should intervene only in religious matters that affected public welfare.

Other writings on toleration were the work of an Anglican layman who sympathized with Puritans, John Milton. In his often cited *Areopagitica*, he pleaded for complete freedom of expression. In two later works — *Of True Religion, Heresy, Schism, and Toleration* and *Of Civil Power in Ecclesiastical Causes* — he undercut the basis for both ecclesiastical and political authority in religious matters. For Protestants, all authority lies in the Scriptures. Heresy is no more than misinterpretation of these. Protestants, Milton argued, can pity heretics for their error, but they cannot persecute them. However, since Roman Catholics do not base their thought on the Scriptures, Protestants do not have to include them in the demand for toleration.

Many dissenters expressed more radical views about religious liberty. An Independent, John Goodwin, favored complete separation of church and state. Governments should exercise no control in the religious sphere, he insisted. They are established solely to direct secular affairs. The abolition of all persecution, said Goodwin, will open the way to discovering truth by the free exchange of ideas and thus to a united understanding.

The fertile discussion of the Commonwealth period did not give birth to genuine liberty or even tolerance in England. That would occur in America. The discussion did set the stage for the birth of religious liberty. As signified by the Act of Toleration, a new spirit was in the air, the spirit of the Enlightenment. In its essence that spirit incorporated a measure of skepticism about religious matters. There is "no such thing as a Christian commonwealth," John

Locke wrote. A church must fend for itself. It will prosper most as a voluntary association. Government has no obligation to it. The responsibility of government is purely civil. The only persons to whom Locke would not grant full tolerance were: (1) persons who "hold opinions contrary to human society," or the immoral; (2) those who claim special privilege that would exempt them from toleration of others (Roman Catholics); (3) those whose religious commitment may make them subversive (Moslems); and (4) atheists, who cannot take an oath.[9] In a later essay, Locke included Jews, Moslems, and pagans, we well as Catholics, Independents, and Quakers, as long as they were law-abiding.

Conclusion

In putting religion on a purely voluntary basis, Locke was speaking for Baptists, Quakers, and many other dissenters. It was precisely this voluntarism that, already as he wrote, had given birth to religious liberty in the American colonies. The long and agonizing labor pains were over.

For Further Reading

Bainton, Roland H. *The Travail of Religious Liberty*. Philadelphia: Westminster Press, 1951.

Bates, M. Searle. *Religious Liberty: An Inquiry*. New York: Harper and Brothers, 1945, pp. 148–86.

Luzzatti, Luigi. *God in Freedom. Studies in the Relations between Church and State*. Translated by Alfonso Arbib-Costa. New York: Macmillan Co., 1930.

For Review

1. Review the sketch of history of religious wars. Discuss how these may have prepared for the growth of tolerance.

2. Review the material about persecutions. Try to put yourself into the context. Discuss both sides of the argument. Where would you have stood during the sixteenth or seventeenth centuries?

3. Put yourself in the place of John Bunyan. Think of your family. Would you have paid the price he did for freedom to preach?

4. Review the factors that led to the development of tolerance and religious liberty. Rank them in order of importance.

5. Review the names of important spokespersons and contributors to religious liberty. Identify the groups with which they belonged. Then ask what part religious considerations played in their concern for liberty.

6. Distinguish again between tolerance and religious liberty. Discuss ways in which the Edict of Nantes in 1598 and Toleration Act in 1689 fell short of religious liberty.

7. Discuss the relationship between the approaches to church and state and religious liberty.

Notes

1. Gaston Bonet-Maury, *Histoire de la liberté de conscience en France, depuis l'Edict de Nantes jusqu'à juillet 1870* (Paris: Alcan, 1900), p. 58.

2. Roland H. Bainton, *The Travail of Religious Liberty* (Philadelphia: Westminster Press, 1951), p. 129.

3. *Reply to Calvin's Book in Which He Endeavors to Show That Heretics Should Be Coerced by the Right of the Sword*, in Bainton, ibid., p. 274.

4. Ibid., p. 279.

5. Article 4 of the Schleitheim Confession; adapted from John C. Wenger, "The Schleitheim Confession of Faith," *Mennonite Quarterly Review* 19 (1945): 249, quoted in George H. Williams, *The Radical Reformation* (Philadelphia: Westminster Press, 1962), p. 183.

6. See Bainton, *The Travail of Religious Liberty*, pp. 123–48.

7. Cited by Sebastian Castellio, *Concerning Heretics*, in ibid., p. 186.

8. Wilbur K. Jordan, *The Development of Religious Toleration in England*, 4 vols. (Cambridge, Mass.: Harvard University Press, 1932–40), 2:274.

9. "First Letter of Toleration," in *Great Books of the Western World* (Chicago: Encyclopaedia Britannica, 1937), pp. 21–22.

Chapter 7

The Long-Awaited Birth

RELIGIOUS LIBERTY was born in America. Many persons assisted in the delivery, but the attending physician was Roger Williams, a "seeker" and briefly a Baptist. The birth was not without complications. Inquisitions, crusades, and other inhuman measures were no longer threatening. But religious establishment was still the pattern in most of the original thirteen colonies. In some of the colonies, up to the drafting of the Bill of Rights in 1791, establishment meant whippings, beatings, arrests, fines, and imprisonment. A few persons lost their lives.

Unpromising Beginnings

Most Americans assume, but erroneously, that America has always had complete religious liberty. One would have expected the first colonists to have guaranteed liberty, for, in most cases, they came to the New World with a conviction that "God hath set before us an open door of liberty." Tolerance did exist in some colonies. In the Middle Colonies — New York, New Jersey, Pennsylvania, and Delaware — the mixture of religious sects virtually assured some tolerance. But these colonies were more the exception than the rule. In New England the Puritans denied others what they coveted for themselves as they sought to implement the Calvinistic idea of a Christian theocracy. In Virginia and the Carolinas Anglicans combined some of Calvin's Puritanism with Elizabeth's way of comprehension. Religious liberty had to find its place of birth in colonies founded on new principles. Those that were most favorable were Catholic Maryland, Rhode Island, and Pennsylvania-Delaware.

The Puritan Establishment: New England

The Pilgrims who landed in Plymouth in 1620 displayed a tolerance that Massachusetts Bay did not adopt. They did not establish Congregationalism by law, and they treated Roger Williams and Anne Hutchinson tolerantly after their exile from the Massachusetts Bay Colony. In addition, church support was voluntary. This tolerance was probably a product of the Pilgrims' stay in Holland and the teachings of their leader John Robinson. Robinson lamented the inconsistency of Protestants who, when persecuted in Roman Catholic countries, demanded liberty but who, when in the majority, would not tolerate others. He concluded that coercion neither pleased God "with unwilling worshipers," nor bettered Christian societies or the coerced.

The Massachusetts Bay pattern, however, prevailed even in Plymouth. When the Puritans came in 1628, they brought with them Calvin's principles of a theocratic society as exemplified by Geneva. The irony of this was that they had fled the English church-state to establish a Puritan church-state. The colonial legislature, the General Court, quickly limited voting privileges to church members. Tests of membership included both Calvinist doctrine and discipline. By 1635 the General Court regulated the affairs of local congregations and judged qualifications of preachers and elders. In 1641 the General Court stated the principle for its involvement in church affairs:

The civil authority . . . . . . hath power and liberty to see the peace, ordinances, and rules of Christ observed in every Church, according to His word. . . . It is the duty of the Christian magistrate to take care that the people be fed with wholesome and sound doctrine.[1]

In 1646 the General Court adopted the Act against Heresy, which imposed a sentence of banishment for persons denying immortality of the soul, resurrection, sin in the unregenerate, the need of repentance, the baptism of infants (for "who shall purposely depart the congregation at the administration of that ordinance"), or leading others to deny these doctrines. The same year, the court made contemptuous conduct toward preachers and nonattendance at church punishable crimes.

The narrow scope of these laws led to several banishments, notably that of Roger Williams and Anne Hutchinson. Anne Hutchinson was condemned for holding meetings in her home where she emphasized grace and direct religious experience rather than what she regarded as a "covenant of works." She fled to Rhode Island in 1638, then to New York, where she was killed by Indians in 1642. Laws enacted against Quakers, who were viewed as "pestilent" heretics, prescribed imprisonment, whipping, hard labor, and banishment. Four Quakers were hanged on Boston Commons when they persisted in returning after banishment. A decree of 1647 required banishment of Catholic priests and then, if they returned, execution. Even when in 1691 a new charter granted liberty of conscience to all Christians, it excluded Papists.

The intolerance of the Massachusetts Bay Colony extended to Plymouth, New Haven, Connecticut, New Hampshire, and, in time, Maine.

The Anglican Establishments: Virginia and the Carolinas

In Virginia and the Carolinas a like intolerance prevailed. Both Massachusetts Bay and Virginia were colonized with similar religious concerns. It was the first duty of Virginians, Captain John Smith declared, to

> preach, baptise into the Christian religion and by the propagation of the Gospel to recover out of the arms of the devil, a number of poor and miserable souls wrapt up unto death in almost invincible ignorance.[2]

The chief difference between the two colonies was the models. Whereas Massachusetts imitated Geneva's theocracy, Virginia imitated England's. In theory, this meant the dominance of the state over the church rather than the reverse. As far as tolerance is concerned, it made little difference. Governor Thomas Dale's "Lawes Divine, Moral and Martial," published in 1612, laid down severe penalties for both theological and ecclesiastical violations. Even though the severity of these was lessened in later decrees, the colony imposed fines for nonattendance at church worship, levied compulsory tithes on every colonist's tobacco, granted a piece of land to every person, built churches by local taxation, and required all ministers to "conform themselves in all things according to canons of the Church of England." The state church arrangement led to banishment of Puritan clergy for refusal to conform, fining and imprisoning and banishing of Quakers, disqualification of Catholics for public office and instant banishment of priests, and penalties for those who refused to allow their children to be baptized.

The Act of Toleration in 1689 alleviated the condition of dissenters and assured liberty of conscience. It did not secure liberty for Roman Catholics, however.

In the Carolinas the need for colonists forced the proprietors to lift some of the narrower regulations of the establishments. Protestant dissenters were granted freedom of conscience and allowed to form their own congregations with ministers of their choice. In Georgia the original charter guaranteed liberty of conscience "to all Persons" and "free exercise of Religion" to all except Roman Catholics. When General Oglethorpe proved unable to maintain the colony, it reverted to the crown. As a result, the Church of England was formally established in 1758.

Pluralism: New York and New Jersey

New York had two establishments, one intolerant, and the other tolerant. Under Dutch rule, despite the liberal policy of the Dutch East India Company, Peter Stuyvesant established and supported the Dutch Reformed Church. Under threat of arrest and imprisonment, he required public contributions to the support of church ministers, required baptism of all children, and allowed baptisms only in a Reformed church. Although at first he permitted only practice of religion according to Dutch Reformed rites, later he made room for Congregationalists and Presbyterians, by no means a major concession. He restrained other denominations. Lutherans were threatened with imprisonment. Baptists were subject to arrest, fines, whipping, and banishment. Quakers, called "instruments of Satan," received even harsher treatment.

When the English captured New Amsterdam in 1664, they showed more leniency but substituted another form of establishment. In effect, the state extended its sway over all denominations. The Duke of York instructed that liberty of conscience be allowed, so long as this would not lead to immoral behavior or disturbance of others in their religion. At the same time he instituted a compulsory subscription in each township for support of ministers to be elected by majority vote of property owners. As in Virginia, he provided for erection of church buildings from public taxes, contributions of all citizens to support of church and state, certificates of ordination of ministers who would be installed by the governor, administration of the Lord's Supper at least once a year by the minister, compulsory baptism of children if the parents requested, and freedom of all from molestation for their religious views. When the Duke of York became King James II in 1685, he attempted to give preference to the Church of England, but only four counties ratified this arrangement.

In New Jersey no denomination held a clear majority. Consequently, efforts of Episcopal clergy to effect an establishment failed.

Free Exercise of Religion:
Rhode Island, Maryland, Pennsylvania, and Delaware

In most of the colonies there were restrictions on the free exercise of religion. At the same time, in some colonies the torch of liberty would be carried. Rhode Island instituted complete liberty. Maryland and Pennsylvania effected a large measure of toleration. In Rhode Island the key was complete separation of church and state.

Maryland came first. This colony was founded in 1632 by Lord Baltimore, a convert to Roman Catholicism. It was a commercial venture, a haven for harassed Catholics, and a base for Catholic missions among the Indians. The royal charter evidently gave Baltimore a free hand in setting religious policy. How much Lord

Baltimore was motivated by concern for religious liberty is uncertain. To attract colonists, however, he opened the door not only to Catholics but to Protestants of all persuasions with a promise of freedom of conscience. The only requirement was belief in Jesus Christ. In 1649 the legislature, at the urging of the third Lord Baltimore, issued a "Toleration Act." This document was far from a declaration of religious liberty, for it ordained the death penalty for blasphemy or denial of the Trinity, and fines for speaking reproachfully about Mary or the apostles or evangelists, for attaching religious labels, and fines and imprisonment for profaning the Lord's Day. It did, however, decree that no person

> professing to believe in Jesus Christ, shall from henceforth be any ways troubled, molested, or discountenanced for, or in respect to, his [or her] religion, nor in the free exercise thereof within this province, or the islands thereunto belonging, nor in any way compelled to believe or exercise any other religion against his [or her] consent, so that they be not unfaithful to the lord proprietary, or molest or conspire against the civil government.[3]

This tolerant policy contained the seeds of its own subversion. Protestants soon outnumbered Roman Catholics. As they did, they took control of the legislature. Already in 1654 the legislature repealed the Toleration Act of 1649. Although Lord Baltimore recovered control and restored toleration in 1658, the fall of James II in 1688 led to the establishment of the Anglican Church as in Virginia. Taxes were collected for its support, Catholic worship was forbidden, and Catholics were refused admission to the colony.

In point of time Rhode Island followed Maryland, but in achievement of religious liberty it went far beyond. The achievement of complete religious liberty, based on the separation of church and state, was due to the efforts of its founder, Roger Williams. Williams was expelled from the Massachusetts Bay Colony in 1635 on the charge that he wanted to separate religious and civil jurisdictions. The express concern of Williams in founding Providence was "to hold forth a lively experiment, that a most flourishing civil State may stand and best be maintained, with a full liberty of religious concernments."[4] After Williams obtained an open charter for his colony from the Earl of Warwick in 1644, the legislature drafted a code that assured the broadest conceivable liberty of conscience and worship. The code concluded with the statement that, except for matters prohibited by the code, "all men may walk as their consciences persuade them, every one in the name of his God."[5] In 1663 Williams obtained from Charles II a charter for the merged colonies of Providence and Rhode Island that, surprisingly, affirmed the freedom of religion.

> No person within the said colony, at any time hereafter, shall be any wise molested, punished, disqualified, or called in question for any difference of opinion in matters of religion; every person may at all times freely and fully enjoy his own judgment and Conscience in matters of religious concernments.[6]

Rhode Island remained true to this charter throughout the seventeenth century. It was not until later that the legislature limited citizenship and eligibility for public office to Protestants.

Pennsylvania and Delaware, originally one colony whose religious policy remained similar, had a tolerant policy but not as far-reaching as that of Rhode Island. In founding a new colony, Penn expressed a desire to found a commonwealth on the cornerstone of freedom as a "holy experiment." He wanted "none to suffer for dissent" and abhorred "obedience to authority without conviction" and the destruction of persons who differed in religious matters. In 1682 he composed and published his "Frame of Government" with its famous declaration that "liberty without obedience is confusion, and obedience without liberty is slavery."[7] The breadth of this general principle, however, was not reflected in the religious section. The "Frame" restricted public offices to "such as profess faith in Jesus Christ."[8] It guaranteed freedom of conscience and of religious profession and practice, and freedom from compulsory worship to all "who confess and acknowledge the one Almighty and Eternal God to be the Creator, Upholder, and Ruler of the world."[9]

The colonial assembly reiterated this provision when it enacted "The Great Law or Body of Laws" in 1682 and added a provision regarding cessation of labor on the Lord's Day "That Looseness in religion, and Atheism may not Creep in under any pretense of Conscience in this Province."[10] This same document stipulated that all civil officers of the province, all deputies to the assembly, and all electors of deputies be professing Christians. Under such provisions, a Jew or non-Christian theist could live in the province but not hold office or vote. An atheist or deist could not even live there. It is notable, against this background, that Roman Catholics could both vote and hold office at first. This right was taken away, however, by the government of William and Mary. From 1703 until 1776 Pennsylvania implemented the requirements of the Act of Toleration of William and Mary, although it did not have an established church.

The Attending Physician

Essentially one colony gave birth to religious liberty in the seventeenth century. Maryland and Pennsylvania, for different reasons, displayed enlightened attitudes, but neither achieved the breadth of freedom that Rhode Island knew. One person was responsible for this "lively experiment." His views merit closer examination.

Roger Williams's concern for religious liberty was grounded in his experience. Born about 1600, he grew to manhood during the years of suppression of dissent by James I and Charles I. The installation of the intolerant William Laud as archbishop of Canterbury in 1628 sent Williams and other Puritans scurrying for freedom in the New World. Laud, an Arminian, was prepared to go to any lengths to suppress Puritanism.

Williams found tolerance equally rare among the Puritans of the Massachusetts Bay Colony when he landed in Boston in 1631. His view that the magistrate had no right to punish breaches of the "first table," that is, the first four Commandments, and his hesitancy to accept communion from the Church of England made a call from the church at Salem welcome. The General Court of the colony, however, blocked his appointment and thus set the course for Williams's subsequent development as an advocate of liberty.

Williams withdrew to Plymouth, where he labored for two years with the approval of Governor Bradford. When he requested dismissal to return to Salem in 1635, however, the Elder Brewster persuaded the church to drop him from communion. He had hardly returned to Salem when John Cotton, destined to be his major opponent in the discussion of religious liberty, landed in Boston. Soon a series of charges were lodged against Williams by the General Court. These led to his banishment from the colony in 1635.

The four particulars under which Williams was banished reflected in essence the foundations upon which he built his argument for religious liberty. The most fundamental was his contention "that the civil magistrate's power extends only to the bodies, and goods, and outward state of men."[11] For Williams, the preservation of liberty depended on complete separation of church and state. In this he was reacting to the Puritan and Anglican concepts of a theocracy in which civil and religious worked in harmony:

> The civil magistrate is only to attend the calling of the civil magistracy concerning the bodies and goods of the subjects, and is himself, if a member of the church and within, subject to the power of the Lord Jesus therein, as any member of the church is, 1 Cor. V.[12]

In 1654 Williams employed an analogy to explain and defend his position against those who contended that his approach to liberty would bind the magistrate's power completely:

> There goes many a ship to sea, with many hundred souls in one ship, whose weal and woe is common, and is a true picture of a commonwealth, or a human combination or society. It hath fallen out sometimes, that both papists and protestants, Jews and Turks, may be embarked in one ship; upon which supposal I affirm, that all the liberty of conscience, that ever I pleaded for, turns upon these two hinges — that none of the papists, protestants, Jews, or Turks, be forced to come to the ship's prayers or worship, nor compelled from their own particular prayers or worship, if they practice any. I further add, that I never denied, that notwithstanding this liberty, the commander of this ship ought to command the ship's course, yea, and also command that justice, peace and

sobriety, be kept and practiced, both among the seamen and all the passengers.[13]

Underlying Williams's concern for the complete independence from secular authority was a conviction, shared with Quakers, Baptists, and other dissenters, that genuine faith must be voluntary. No amount of coercion can win any to God. All it can do is encourage hypocrisy, a carnal repentance. Only one means can be employed in obtaining a conversion, the word of God. In summarizing his theses at the beginning of *The Bloudy Tenent of Persecution*, Williams showed how far he would press the voluntary principle:

> It is the will and command of God that, since the coming of his Son the Lord Jesus, a permission of the most Paganish, Jewish, Turkish, or anti-Christian consciences and worships be granted to all men in all nations and countries; and they are only to be fought against with that sword which is only, in soul matters, able to conquer: to wit, the sword of God's Spirit, the word of God.[14]

Against this backdrop Williams, like the Anabaptists, believed that the true church, the church of the Spirit, should be clearly separated from this world. This conviction evidently caused him to refuse communion with the Anglican Church and, for a time, even to withdraw communion from his wife. More significantly, it fed his attack on the Puritan theocracy. There can be no Christian commonwealth. The union between church and state that Constantine effected caused harm rather than good. When the church is the true, regenerate people of God, it will suffer persecution, not inflict it, Williams declared. It must never lower its standards so that it may embrace all persons within a certain nation.

Williams argued for separation of church and state, as Roland Bainton has pointed out, not simply because "the spheres of their operation are distinct" but because "their respective memberships must be different."[15] This line of thought would have important repercussions for the future, for it opened the door to the complete secularization of the state. Although many have lauded the principle of separation for its guarantees regarding religious liberty, others have asked whether Williams carried it too far. The issue that must be raised is whether a people can or should distinguish so confidently the civil and the religious spheres. Three centuries of American history confirm that, on this point, Williams was too self-confident. At the same time, however, they prove the truth of his main insight, that religion does not require the support of the civil powers, whether by coercion, taxation, or other helps, in order to survive. Voluntarism in religion will work.

Awkward Infancy

The infant that Williams delivered was healthy enough, but many factors threatened it during infancy. The Massachusetts Bay Colony tried to strangle Rhode Island commercially by refusing access to Boston harbor. In 1665 a Rhode Island bill outlawed the Quakers for refusal to bear arms, but it never became law. The shift in the English monarchy in 1689 brought pressures to conform to provisions of the Act of Toleration by denying citizenship to Roman Catholics.

Despite these and other pressures, religious liberty did survive in Rhode Island. The "lively experiment," however, scarcely influenced other colonies until after the American Revolution. On the eve of the American Revolution, Rhode Island stood alone as a free colony in the midst of various types of establishments. Still, as Leo Pfeffer has stated in *Church, State, and Freedom*, in the century between Williams's death and the adoption of the Bill of Rights, the growth of liberty was being prepared for by both practical and ideological factors.

Among important practical factors were the issuing of the Act of Toleration by William and Mary in 1689, the multiplicity of sects that migrated to the English colonies of America, the large number of unchurched persons during the period between the American Revolution and the adoption of the First Amendment, the rise of commerce, and the tendency of the Revolution itself to unify the people and to submerge differences. Among important ideological factors were influences such as the Williams-Penn experiments, John Locke's social contract theory, the revival movement of the mid-eighteenth century known as the Great Awakening, and rationalism and Deism.

It would be impossible to trace the effect of each of these factors on the growth of religious liberty. For the purposes of this study some of the coordinate effects of them can be illustrated by focusing on the struggle for disestablishment in New England and Virginia in which Baptists played an important role. "The Baptists," Pfeffer has said, "were the most active of all the colonial religious bodies in their unceasing struggle for religious freedom and separation."[16]

In Virginia the Church of England retained its established status up to the Revolution. Dissenters, especially Baptists and Presbyterians, often experienced the lash of persecution and organized their opposition. Since they represented half to two-thirds of the population after the Great Awakening, they carried much weight. The Revolution strengthened their cause, for, while Anglicans usually fought on the royalist side, dissenters fought on the colonial side. At the same time Virginia's political leaders — Washington, Patrick Henry, George Mason, James Madison, and Thomas Jefferson — generally accepted the social contract theory and leaned toward Deism, a faith that substituted rational religion for revealed religion.

These men had much sympathy for the dissenters' cause. Jefferson especially spoke eloquently of "liberty of conscience" as a "natural right" that not only should not but could not be surrendered to a civil official. "Reason and free inquiry are the only effectual agents against error. Give a loose to them, they will support the true religion by bringing every false one to their tribunal, to the test of their investigation. They are the natural enemies of error, and of error only."[17] While in Philadelphia to draft the Declaration of Independence, he included in a draft of a proposed constitution for Virginia the statement that "all persons shall have full and free liberty of religious opinion; nor shall any be compelled to frequent or maintain any religious institution."[18]

The Virginia establishment did not topple immediately. Pressures from Baptists, Presbyterians, and Lutherans and the statesmanship of Mason, Madison, and Jefferson, however, little by little chipped away the foundations. In December 1776 the legislature passed a compromise bill that repealed the laws punishing heresy and absence from worship and those requiring dissenters to contribute to the establishment. Baptists, Presbyterians, and other dissenters found this unacceptable and pressed for complete abolition of state support of religion.

In 1791 John Leland, a Baptist minister who had the ear of Jefferson and Madison, stated the dissenting view exactly: "Government has no more to do with the religious opinions of men than it has with the principle of mathematics."[19] In 1784 the dissenters, led by Baptists, fought the passage of a bill drafted by Patrick Henry that would have required a general tax "for the support of the Christian religion, or of some Christian church, denomination or communion of Christians, or for some form of Christian worship."[20] James Madison led opposition in the legislature. In 1785 his "Memorial and Remonstrance on the Religious Rights of Man," which laid down both practical and ideological reasons why government could not interfere in religious affairs, turned the tide against the Henry bill. It cleared the way for adoption of Jefferson's "An Act for Establishing Religious Freedom," introduced first in 1779 but passed finally in 1786. After that only vestiges of the old establishment remained, the last being removed in 1802.

In New England a similar struggle for disestablishment of the Puritan theocracy occurred. The chief leader there was a Baptist pastor named Isaac Backus. In 1772 the Warren Association employed him as an agent to represent Baptists in their relations with the Massachusetts Bay Colony. Like Roger Williams and most other Baptists, he based his pleas not only on practical grounds but also on the ideological ground that the state lacks the capacity to meddle in religious affairs. He vigorously contested the Massachusetts precinct tax in support of the established church with the declaration that "religion is a concern between God and the soul with which no human authority can intermeddle."[21] He was arrested for refusal to pay.

When the Continental Congress met in Philadelphia in 1774, Backus presented the plea of Baptists, Quakers, and Presbyterians to the Massachusetts delegation. John Adams warned him that his pleas likely would go unheeded. In Massachusetts, however, the constitution of 1780, while affirming that worship of the Supreme Being is a duty, decreed that no person should be molested "for worshipping God in the manner and season most agreeable to the dictates of his own conscience . . . provided he does not disturb the public peace or obstruct others in their religious worship." Similarly, while providing for public support of the teaching of religion, it decreed that all denominations would receive equal support. "And every denomination of Christians, demeaning themselves peaceable, and as good subjects of the commonwealth, shall be equally under the protection of the law; and no subordination of any one sect or denomination to another shall ever be established by law."[22]

Backus, who continued his pleas until his death in 1806, and others of his persuasion won an even greater victory in the addition of a Bill of Rights to the newly framed Constitution of the United States. As Pfeffer has pointed out, the Constitutional Convention of 1787 displayed a much less religious overtone than the Continental Congress had. The Constitution itself omitted reference to God. Thus criticism came from two sides as state legislatures considered ratification. On the one side, those concerned for a religious influence on society feared lest irreligion prevail. In Massachusetts, for example, legislators foresaw the opening of a door to Jews, Turks, and infidels. On the other side, persons who were more strongly concerned for liberty wanted further guarantees against state interference in religion.

The omission of such guarantees nearly prevented ratification. North Carolina and Rhode Island refused to ratify the Constitution until a bill of rights was adopted to assure religious freedom and disestablishment. Six other states ratified it but proposed amendments to guarantee religious liberty. Some persons, for example, Alexander Hamilton, argued that a bill of rights was unnecessary. Many others, including Jefferson, presented the other side. In 1789, shortly after his election to the House of Representatives, James Madison introduced the articles for a proposed bill of rights. Passed in that year by both the House and the Senate, the Bill of Rights was ratified by the required number of states in 1791.

The original ten amendments to the Constitution began and ended with guarantees concerning religious liberty. The First Amendment decreed that "Congress shall make no law respecting an establishment of religion, or prohibiting the free exercise thereof." Article VI of the Constitution directed that " . . . no religious test shall ever be required as a qualification to any office or public trust under the United States."

Religious liberty had not only survived, it had grown. The question at this point was: Would it be more than a paper dream? Would religion survive without the civil power's support? Would the society maintain integrity if religion was confined to the private sphere?

Two centuries of American history leave mixed impressions and answers. Religion, especially Christianity, has survived. Indeed, it seems to have thrived without the support of government. Any observer of American history can see, however, that complete separation of church and state is neither possible nor desirable. The separation is always relative. In most of its history the American Republic has maintained a high degree of separateness, but the American people have recognized to varying degrees the necessary benefits of religion in their society. Many are asking whether religion has had enough impact. *Does a new understanding of religious liberty need to be framed, one that does not use Williams's model of absolute separation of church and state?* That may be the most pressing issue in modern America.

For Further Reading

Bainton, Roland H. *The Travail of Religious Liberty*. Philadelphia: Westminster Press, 1951, pp. 208–28.

Cobb, Sanford H. *The Rise of Religious Liberty in America*. New York: Macmillan Co., 1902.

Miller, Glenn T. *Religious Liberty in America: History and Prospects*. Philadelphia: Westminster Press, 1976.

Miller, William Lee. *The First Liberty: Religion and the American Republic*. New York: Knopf, 1986.

Pfeffer, Leo. *Church, State, and Freedom*. Rev. ed. Boston: Beacon Press, 1967, pp. 71–127.

For Review

1. Evaluate the popular assumption that America has always had religious liberty.

2. Discuss the similarities and differences of the different types of establishment of religion in the early colonies.

3. Compare religious freedom or tolerance in the three colonies that came closest to giving birth to religious liberty — Maryland, Rhode Island, and Pennsylvania-Delaware. What significant difference did the Rhode Island experiment have?

4. Review Roger Williams's theory of religious liberty. What are its strengths? What question does it leave unanswered? Why did the other colonies not adopt it immediately?

5. Review the practical and ideological factors that prepared for the adoption of religious liberty and separation of church and state after the American Revolution.

6. What part did Baptists play in the development of religious liberty?

7. Why did persons like Isaac Backus and Thomas Jefferson want a Bill of Rights added to the Constitution? What did the Bill of Rights do to assure religious liberty?

8. Discuss the questions raised at the end of the chapter.

Notes

1. Leo Pfeffer, *Church, State, and Freedom*, rev. ed. (Boston: Beacon Press, 1967), p. 75.

2. Evarts B. Greene, *Religion and the State* (New York: New York University Press, 1941), p. 32.

3. Sanford H. Cobb, *The Rise of Religious Liberty in America* (New York: Macmillan Co., 1902), p. 376.

4. Cited in ibid., p. 423.

5. Cited in ibid., p. 431.

6. Cited in ibid., p. 436.

7. Cited in ibid., p. 442.

8. Sec. 34 of "Frame of Government" as cited in ibid.

9. Sec. 35 of "Frame of Government" as cited in ibid.

10. From "The Great Law or Body of Laws" as cited in ibid, p. 443.

11. Edward Bean Underhill, ed., *Roger Williams' "The Bloudy Tenent of Persecution" and "Mr. Cotton's Letter Examined and Answered"*, ed. for the Hanserd Knollys Society (London: J. Haddon, 1848), p. 375.

12. Ibid., p. 326.

13. Williams's letter "To the Town of Providence," cited by Anson Phelps Stokes, *Church and State in the United States* (New York: Harper and Bros., 1950), 1:197.

14. Underhill, *"The Bloudy Tenent of Persecution,"* p. 2.

15. Roland H. Bainton, *The Travail of Religious Liberty* (Philadelphia: Westminster Press, 1951), p. 223.

16. Pfeffer, *Church, State and Freedom*, p. 99.

17. Joseph L. Blau, ed., *Cornerstones of Religious Freedom in America* (Boston: Beacon Press, 1949), p. 78.

18. Cited by Saul K. Padover, *The Complete Jefferson* (New York: Duell, Sloan & Peace, 1943), p. 109.

19. John Leland, *Rights of Conscience and Therefore Religious Opinions Not Cognizable by Law*, in John M. Mecklin, *The Story of American Dissent* (New York: Harcourt, Brace and Co., 1934), p. 297.

20. H. J. Eckenrode, *Separation of Church and State in Virginia* (Richmond: Virginia State Library, 1910), p. 86.

21. Cited by Edward F. Humphrey, *Nationalism and Religion in America, 1774–1789* (Boston: Chipman Law Publishing Co., 1924), pp. 331–32.

22. Francis N. Thorpe, *Federal and State Constitutions, Colonial Charters and Other Organic Laws* (Washington: Government Printing Office, 1909), 3:1889–90.

Chapter 8

Religious Liberty Today

THE STORY of religious liberty's birth has been told. It would not be appropriate, however, to stop with its infancy, for its survival depends on continuous and unfailing vigilance. Some attention must be given to its present condition in America. This condition will be described first in terms of church-state relations, next in terms of the free exercise of religion, and finally in terms of an important gain for religious liberty in the Second Vatican Council of the Roman Catholic Church.

Church and State in America

"A Wall of Separation"?

When Thomas Jefferson interpreted the First Amendment, he spoke of "a wall of separation." His phrase has been repeated many times as the courts of the United States of America have sought to apply the Constitution's provision for religious liberty. Little reflection is required, however, to convince one that the phrase is metaphorical and not a literal description of church-state relations. Hundreds of intricate court decisions prove that church and state intermingle at many points. They overlap geographically. They have some of the same constituency, the state merely having more. They have a mutual concern for the well-being of all the people of the nation. They have a stake in many of the same institutions. They are mutually concerned for morality and good citizenship. What, then, could Jefferson have meant by "a wall of separation" and how does this concept apply today?

Jefferson, along with many of this nation's founding fathers, was much influenced by the Enlightenment view that religion is a "purely private matter." To him, separation meant the complete disengagement of the church from the state and the state from the church except through the private individual. He would not have envisioned the vast array of institutions that religious groups in America have developed to foster their diverse goals. Correspondingly, he would not have anticipated the many cases concerning church and state that have arisen almost exclusively from the institutional side of religion. Were religion solely a matter of conscience, few problems would have arisen, for governments cannot control the conscience. Since religion also involves expression, assembly, and corporate activities, many problems have occurred and will continue to occur.

Because religion expresses itself institutionally, separation of church and state has meant reasonable or adequate rather than the absolute separation that Jefferson's phrase seems to imply. Separation is not equivalent to religious liberty. It is conceivable that a nation might use a policy of absolute separation to deny religious freedom, as Marxist countries do. The long-range goal of such countries is a totally secular state, devoid of religious influence. Religion is carefully restricted and controlled according to the government's intermediate aims. To obtain lend-lease aid from the United States during World War II, Stalin relented briefly in his efforts to wipe out the churches of the Soviet Union. When the war was over, he tightened the restrictions again.

The American policy of church-state separation, by way of contrast, does not seek the total secularization of the state, although a small minority of persons, represented for instance by avowed atheist Madalyn Murray O'Hair, may desire that. The policy seeks another goal, complete religious liberty insofar as the exercise of religion does not interfere with the welfare of the citizens of a state. In practice there has been more mutual helpfulness than antagonism between church and government at various levels. This mutual helpfulness has produced possible violations of the First and Tenth Amendments. Such cases constantly test the tautness of the line that separates church and state.

Violations of the First Amendment have occurred at local or state levels more often than at the national level. This is a result of several factors. One is the strong majority that certain religious groups hold in some areas. In American politics majority sentiment often guides decisions favoring majority views. The average voters cannot or will not distinguish their religious from their political views. The tendency is toward adoption of laws that favor a certain church or its views and tend in effect to "establish" one religion, the majority religion. In some states "blue laws" have favored Christian sentiments over Jewish. In others prohibition of distribution of information on birth control has favored Roman Catholic over Protestant or other religious views. For years such violations may go unnoticed until a person or group who feel the inequity take the matter to court.

Another factor is a difference of opinion whether the Bill of Rights applies to state or local governments. The First Amendment stated expressly that "Congress shall make no law. . . . " Even after ratification of these amendments in 1791, it was some time before all states eliminated their establishments. Not until passage of the Fourteenth Amendment in 1868 did the Constitution itself offer a fairly clear basis for applying the First Amendment to the states. In its relevant portion, the Fourteenth Amendment stipulated:

> No State shall make or enforce any law which shall abridge the privileges or immunities of citizens of the United States; nor shall any State deprive any person of life, liberty, or property without due process of law; nor deny to any person within its jurisdiction the equal protection of the laws.

Although this amendment did not mention religion specifically, it has been interpreted as making the Bill of Rights applicable to the states.

The Taut Line

The preceding information should dispel the false notion that the separation of church and state has been faultlessly maintained in

America. Its maintenance has required great effort by many interested persons and groups. Overlaps sometimes have posed grave dangers to religious liberty. To sharpen one's perception of the issue, it will be helpful to examine a number of places where the overlap has been a problem.

One place is *state aid to religion*. Such aid has taken the form of direct governmental grants to religious bodies, grants to denominational welfare institutions, involvement of churches in Peace Corps and antipoverty programs sustained by governmental funds, allowing church usage of state property, tax exemption of church property and clergy, special postage rates for religious literature, and reduced rates for utilities and transportation. Apart from direct aid, the legality of these forms of aid is by no means clear from the many court decisions that have tested them. The complexity and expense of the American judicial process often has inhibited testing. Americans owe a great debt to both secular and religious organizations for the many cases that do go to court to keep the line taut.

A second place where overlap occurs is *church involvement in state affairs*. Some American religious groups, including many Baptists, have avoided involvement in public affairs as a matter of principle. This policy, however, is more characteristic of minority groups with strong sectarian tendencies, for example, the Mennonite Amish. As most sects or religious groups have prospered in America, they have developed a social consciousness and, correspondingly, become more involved in social affairs.

The most evident involvement is in politics. From the beginning of the nation, the clergy have held positions in government. The Constitution guarantees that right. Churches have frequently led the nation in social causes: temperance, emancipation of slaves, prison reform, prohibition, peace, campaigns against pornography, racial justice, civil rights, women's rights, and many others. They have sustained references to God in official statements, for example, "In God We Trust" on coins. Some groups have sought unsuccessfully to have references to Christ included in official statements. Many Americans think of America as a Christian nation. The nation has given public recognition to the place of religion by way of congressional and military chaplains, oath-taking in courts, and the national census. Vigilance has been required to prevent the imposing of religious tests for public office.

A third place where overlap occurs is *state involvement in church affairs*. This involvement is evident in proclamation of thanksgiving days and special days of prayer or fasting, in so-called blue laws, in state intervention into ecclesiastical disputes, for example, regarding church property, and in President Truman's appointment of an ambassador to the Vatican in 1951.

Religion and Public Education

Much of the debate regarding church-state separation has focused on religion and public education. At the beginning of the nation's history, education was directed largely by the churches. Although Boston established a public school as early as 1635, it was under church supervision. The first nationwide provision for public schools was made by the Northwest Ordinance of 1787. The freeing of public school education from sectarianism came later, largely through efforts of Horace Mann in Massachusetts, appointed secretary of the first state education board in 1837. Mann favored religious education but taught in such a way as to exclude denominational bias. So long as America remained almost exclusively Protestant, this posed no problem. As Catholic and Jewish populations grew through immigration, problems arose and led to the secularization of public schools. Protestants preferred to see all religious instruction removed from public school education rather than allow the teaching of Catholic doctrine in the schools. In some parts of the nation, especially the South, religion has retained an impact, but the impact has been small.

Americans with a religious commitment have never been happy with the secularization of education. Roman Catholics have long decried the "secular" character of public schools and have maintained in opposition a complete system of parochial schools. Protestants have proposed alternatives to elimination of all religious education: teaching Protestantism and excusing non-Protestants, separate teaching of each faith, school credit for outside religious teaching, teaching the "common core" of the major faiths, objective teaching "about" religion, and teaching "moral and spiritual values." All of these proposals, however, have run into problems. The one alternative that has received cautious sanction at the Supreme Court level has been released time instruction. By this plan children who desire religious instruction are freed from regular classes to attend religion classes elsewhere. Some persons view even this arrangement as a threat to separation of church and state.

At various times other religious practices have been introduced into the public schools. Most have been declared unconstitutional on the grounds that they represent sectarian viewpoints. One such practice is *Bible reading*. In 1963 the Supreme Court decided that exclusion of Bible reading does not violate anyone's constitutional rights. It has not yet decided, however, whether inclusion of Bible reading would do so. Most state court decisions have sustained Bible reading on the grounds that the Bible in the King James Version is not a sectarian book. A few state courts, however, have come to the reverse conclusion and thus excluded reading of the Bible.

Another is *prescribed prayers*. In a celebrated case the Supreme Court ruled against a supposedly "nonsectarian" prayer prescribed by the New York State Board of Regents in 1951 for daily recitation in public schools. The Court interpreted the enforcement of the practice as a violation of the establishment clause in the First Amendment. An effort by Congressman Frank Becker of New York to introduce an amendment to the Constitution that would permit prayer recitation, Bible reading, or both in public schools failed to obtain the necessary signatures in Congress.

Certain other religious practices have occurred in public schools from time to time with questionable legality. These include: holy day celebrations such as Christmas, joint holy day celebrations such as Hanukkah and Christmas, nuns in habits teaching in public schools, and baccalaureate services. The teaching of religion in state universities has received clearance insofar as the study promotes objective understanding rather than belief and does not involve compulsory chapel attendance.

The most disputed question relating to the educational sphere has to do with *state aid to parochial schools*. With an extensive and increasingly costly system of parochial schools, the Roman Catholic Church has sought in various ways to obtain state aid. Beginning with the refusal of the New York state legislature in 1842, however, many states have turned down such requests. Every state admitted to the United States since 1876 has been forced by Congress to bar aid to parochial schools in its constitution. Although states have occasionally violated the provision, the Supreme Court has ruled in several well-known cases that the First Amendment bars direct aid to parochial schools. The famous Everson versus Board of Education case in 1947 ruled that government funds could be used to transport children to parochial schools but denied other aid. The McCollum versus Board of Education case in 1948 held that the use of public school property for religious education violated the First Amendment. The Zorach versus Clauson case of 1951 specifically said, "Government may not finance religious groups."

An alternative approach to obtaining government aid has been *the incorporation of a parochial school system into the public system.* This plan, tried first at Faribault, Minnesota, in 1892, had a precedent in the early incorporation of Protestant schools into the public system. Whereas the latter resulted in the complete secularization of the schools, the Faribault plan intended to complete religious instruction in the schools after regular school hours. A number of courts have ruled against the plan. Despite such rulings, many local school systems have adopted such arrangements. The schools are in effect controlled by the Roman Catholic Church.

Several other approaches to obtaining state aid have been indirect. These include furnishing secular textbooks for use by parochial school children, transportation to parochial schools at public expense, and shared-time or dual enrollment in public and parochial schools. Each of these has received cautious approval by the courts. Whether any of them violates the Constitution may depend on how it is implemented.

Finally, aid has been sought from the federal government. Since the Northwest Ordinance of 1787, the federal government has shown a keen interest in education. Inclusion of nonpublic schools in federal grants to education did not pose a problem until Catholic opposition halted passage of a series of bills granting federal aid to general education between 1881 and 1890. Subsequently, Roman Church opposition barred several other acts. In the late 1930s, however, the church modified its stance in the hope of obtaining aid for parochial schools. To obtain passage of other bills, legislators eventually included the latter in grants for essential school services, such as transportation, nonreligious textbooks and supplies, and health and welfare services. A series of bills opened the way for the rather liberal provisions of the Elementary and Secondary Education Act of 1965. The latter, designed to aid the deprived, made services available to nonpublic as well as public school children in such a way as to leave serious questions about the separation of church and state.

The Free Exercise of Religion

What has been said thus far concerns chiefly those ways in which Americans have avoided an establishment of religion, that is, putting one group in a favored position. This has been achieved largely by holding a taut line of separation. Still to be considered, however, are the boundaries for free exercise of religion. As indicated earlier, boundaries would hardly need to be set were religion a strictly private and inwardly personal matter detached from civil life. Since it also involves expression, assembly, and corporate activities, however, it enjoys at best a qualified freedom. Boundaries set by the state often bring conflict between church and state. They go beyond the constitutional limits set on state power when they trespass on the religious conscience. Where the line marking trespass lies is as difficult to establish as is the line between church and state. Several areas present difficulties.

National Defense and Unity

One such view is *national defense and unity*. In general the courts have taken the view that religion should be exercised freely so long as its exercise poses no "clear and present danger" to national security. The principle is roughly the same as that of free speech that forbids one to cry "Fire!" in a crowded theater. It has frequently been tested with reference to conscientious objection to military service on religious grounds. Right of conscientious objection has been established not on the basis of the Constitution but by public legislation. Congress has seen no serious threat to national security in exempting conscientious objectors. However, the Vietnam war posed this issue in a more serious form as thousands of youth exercised the right of objecting on grounds of conscience not originally defined by the word "religion." Court decisions have recognized the broader definition of religion, but they have not approved selective conscientious objection.

The principle has been tested also by refusal of Jehovah's Witnesses, on religious grounds, to salute the American flag. Doing so, in their minds, violated the prohibition of the Second Commandment against making "graven images." In 1940 the Supreme Court ruled against them on the grounds that freedom of conscience is not unlimited and that saluting the flag aided national unity. After a series of widespread incidents in which Jehovah's Witnesses suffered grave abuses, in 1943 the Court reversed the previous decision. This time it rejected the earlier conclusion that national unity could be effected by force. Although the majority opinion admitted that religious liberty was not absolute, it saw in coercion to salute the flag the opening of a door to more serious coercion. Thus it assured broad limits for religious expression.

Domestic Tranquillity

Another area that causes difficulty in deciding the lines of trespass on religious freedom is that of *keeping orderliness in society*. The state is responsible for protecting public morality, keeping peace, protecting citizens from slander, regulating use of public property, protecting and regulating private property, and preventing fraud. Sometimes religious activities create conflicts regarding these responsibilities. Obviously there are limits to the exercise of religion when activities affect the maintenance of an orderly society. Once again, however, the boundaries are not easily determined, and the courts have tended to set the limits as far out as possible.

In the matter of *public morality*, the most noted example of limitation was prohibition of polygamy among Mormons. In Mormonism polygamy was viewed originally as a religious obligation. In 1878 when the Supreme Court prohibited multiple marriages as "odious among the northern and western nations of Europe, and, until the establishment of the Mormon church, . . . almost exclusively a feature of the life of Asiatic and of African people," it virtually made the Mormon religion illegal. The strengthening of this decision in 1890 to allow punishment of a person merely for being a member of a sect that permitted polygamy led the Mormons to adopt a declaration of submission to federal law. Polygamy has not disappeared entirely among Mormons, however, and conservative Mormons have subsequently suffered for violations of state or federal laws.

In *keeping the public peace*, Jehovah's Witnesses have tested the limits of free exercise of religion more severely than any other groups. The aggressive and polemical nature of their mission work has led frequently to local restrictions upon their witnessing. It has involved especially bitter attacks on Roman Catholicism. A number of Supreme Court cases have established general guidelines, as summarized by Leo Pfeffer:

1. The First Amendment guarantees the right to preach and teach religion in the public streets and parks.

2. The states have the constitutional power to restrict street preaching where such action is clearly and immediately necessary to preserve the public peace.

3. This constitutional power includes the power to punish "verbal acts," such as expletives and "fighting words."

4. It does not include the power to prohibit street meetings by sects or individuals whose preachings may incite an outbreak of disorder because of their attacks on other religions or because of their intemperate language.

5. Nor does it include the power to confer on a public official unbridled or broad discretion to grant or withhold as he sees fit the permits necessary for street or park meetings.[1]

Similar problems have arisen recently in connection with the Black Muslims. The extremist views of some Black Muslims have caused officials to impose restrictions. Complaints have come especially from prisoners. Prison officials have generally sought to avoid interference with Black Muslim religious practices, but conflicts have nevertheless arisen with regard to some of these (such as refusal to eat pork).

In *protecting citizens from slander*, local and state governments have composed laws against blasphemy and sacrilege. Such laws set limits to freedom of expression about religion through various media and have not been upheld by the Supreme Court.

In *regulating the use of public property*, broad limits have been set for religious activities. Although local and state governments have often placed severe restrictions upon certain groups, the Supreme Court has insisted on almost complete freedom for religious speeches, assemblies, and activities. Several decisions have ruled that local ordinances may not prohibit soliciting or distributing handbills for religious purposes because to do so might prevent riots, disturbances, or disorderly assembly. There must first be a real danger to the civil order. At the same time, until recently, the Supreme Court has seen no constriction of the free exercise of religion in refusal to make public buildings available to religious groups. The state may not grant free use of public buildings for religious purposes, because such would violate separation of church and state. A ruling of the U.S. Supreme Court, however, decreed that public schools must permit use of school facilities to religious groups on the same basis that they allow their use for other organizations.

In *protecting and regulating private property*, court decisions also have insisted upon a wide range for the exercise of religion. Private property rights have been protected carefully in America. But these are not so unlimited that they might prohibit "invasion" by religious groups, for example, by leaflets and loud speakers. While the courts have upheld zoning regulations that would allow only residences in one area, thus prohibiting churches, they have stricken those that would forbid building of churches in a whole town. The reasoning is that so long as persons could travel short distances to church, their freedom would not suffer.

In *preventing fraud*, the courts have been hesitant to restrict religious activities. The general rule for testing fraud is the sincerity of belief of the person or group charged with fraud. Sincerity of belief is difficult to test. But the rule does lean heavily toward preservation of the free exercise of religion.

The General Welfare

A final area in which the limits of free exercise of religion are difficult to set is that involving preservation of the health and well-being of the people. Here religious views and practices often conflict with legitimate state concerns: public health, regulation of marriage, the welfare of children, social welfare, and taxation for support of public services.

As regards *public health*, the courts have usually upheld the rights of government to regulate health even when this results in restrictions on religious practices. In 1905 the Supreme Court ruled that committees could force vaccination against smallpox in the face of a threatened epidemic. In 1943 the Court cited the ruling when it decided that one "cannot claim freedom from compulsory vaccination...on religious grounds." In 1952 the Supreme Court reached a similar decision regarding examination of college students for tuberculosis, an examination opposed by Christian Scientists.

The courts have placed the saving of life above religious scruples in individual cases also. In one instance a Chicago family court, sustained by the Illinois Supreme Court, ordered a blood transfusion for an infant against objections of the parents, who were Jehovah's Witnesses. Suicide on the basis of religious scruples has been prevented.

As regards *marriage*, a number of governmental statutes override religious scruples. These include laws favoring monogamy, requirements concerning premarital blood tests for venereal diseases, state marriage licenses, and circulation of information about contraception and family planning.

As regards *the welfare of children*, government controls have occasionally taken precedence over religious scruples in special instances. A fairly clear case is that where certain religious activities, for example, solicitation or witnessing by children of Jehovah's Witnesses, may endanger the children's health. The courts have moved more hesitantly to interfere with rights of parents in the religious upbringing of a child or to interpose the issue of religion in determining child custody or adoption. They have been rather forceful, however, in imposing state regulations regarding education on the Old Order Amish. The Amish, on religious grounds, withdraw their children from public school at age fourteen. The Supreme Court of Pennsylvania upheld a state law that required that all children attend school until age seventeen.

As regards *social welfare*, several questions have been raised. One is the legality of requiring all persons to participate in social security programs. Another is whether persons who refuse to work on Saturday can be disqualified from unemployment benefits.

As regards *taxation*, numerous problems have been posed regarding exemptions for religious organizations. Generally speaking, states have granted exemptions rather freely. They may not tax exclusively religious practices, such as preaching, or primarily religious practices, such as sale of religious literature. They may tax practices that require regulation in the interest of public order or safety, purely commercial transactions, and the income of clergy.

Roman Catholicism and Religious Liberty

This brief glance at religious liberty in America today shows a child alive and well as a result of continuous attention by many persons. The happy experience of America has found admirers in other parts of the world. A few nations have both adopted separation of church and state and guaranteed the free exercise of religion along American lines. In many other countries, however, religious liberty is in serious travail. In some there are scant prospects of its birth in the foreseeable future.

Religious liberty's hopes for the future are bound up with what is happening in Christianity today. The prospects are good. The Roman Catholic Church has added its voice to that of other denominations that have long cried out for complete liberty. The Second Vatican Council (1962–65) represented an important breakthrough in the Roman Catholic attitude toward religious freedom.

Prior to the council, the church's official policy opposed separation of church and state and sought, where possible, an establishment of Roman Catholicism. This policy harked back to the Middle Ages when the church was established in all the nations of Europe. It experienced severe testing in the later Middle Ages with the rise of nationalism. As the papacy weakened about 1300, nationalists, particularly in France, attacked first the pope's involvement in secular affairs, then his dominance in spiritual affairs. Between 1307 and 1377 the papacy, transferred to Avignon in France, fell under the sway of the French monarchy. The papal reaction was to reassert more fiercely the prerogatives of the church.

The Protestant Reformation served to heighten further the church's determination not to loose its control any further. The Council of Trent ended in 1563 with a declaration that salvation depended absolutely on submission to the bishop of Rome.

The church's response to growing nationalism, rationalism, and indifference during the nineteenth and early twentieth centuries was reactionary. The popes responded to these with further assertions of papal authority. Such assertions reached a peak during the reign of Pius IX (1846–78). At first responding with openness to liberal currents, Pius became increasingly conservative. In 1864 he published the famous *Syllabus of Errors*, condemning separation of church and state, public education, and "latitudinarianism," the belief that one faith (Protestantism) is as good as another (Roman Catholicism). In 1869 he convened the First Vatican Council, which made papal infallibility a dogma of the church.

Although this conservatism tended to prevail until the Second Vatican Council, some cracks began to appear. Pius IX's successor, Leo XIII, turned Catholics' attention toward modern social concerns in the famous encyclical *Rerum Novarum*. He also encouraged biblical studies. A movement known as "modernism" developed. Although forcefully stamped out in 1907, this movement opened some windows to modern critical thought as found in Protestantism. Then in Nazi concentration camps during World War II, both Catholics and Protestants began to discover that they had much in common and needed to work together.

In 1958 Pope John XXIII brought many of these new perceptions together. He began to call Protestants "separated brethren" and to open the door for Catholic and Protestant dialogue. He manifested concern for suffering humanity everywhere. Finally, he convened the Second Vatican Council as a means of implementing three goals: (1) "updating" the church, (2) improving its effectiveness in fulfilling the Christian mission, and (3) restoring the relationship with other Christians. With such goals as these it was inevitable that one specific concern of the council would be religious liberty, for none of the other goals could be met without it.

The Declaration on Religious Freedom involved "the greatest argument on religious freedom" in the history of the church.[2] Although presented during the first session of the council in 1962, it did not win approval until 1965. The council struggled hard to free itself from centuries of teaching that supported constraint in religious beliefs and practice. The finished product, however, gave a strong base for complete liberty not only of conscience but also of proclamation, assembly, and activities.

The declaration began with an acknowledgment of the growth of a sense of human worth and the corresponding demand for freedom from coercion. Although it asserted that the "one true religion subsists in the catholic and apostolic Church, to which the Lord Jesus committed the duty of spreading it abroad among all men" (see Matt. 28:19–20), and that all persons are bound to seek the truth revealed in it, the council rejected coercion as a means of fulfilling this mission. It asserted that religious freedom is a natural human right that makes the person or groups immune to pressures to adopt views that would be contrary to their beliefs or to pressures that would restrain them from acting in accordance with these beliefs. Both revelation and reason establish a foundation for the doctrine of human dignity on which religious freedom rests. Persons cannot act in accordance with their own nature, "unless they enjoy immunity from external coercion as well as psychological freedom." God created persons free to seek truth according to conscience. The freedom that applies to individuals also applies to groups, for both human beings and religion are social by nature. So long as individuals or groups observe "just requirements of public order," they should have freedom to

> govern themselves according to their own norms, honor the Supreme Being in public worship, assist their members in the practice of the religious life, strengthen them by instruction, and promote institutions in which they may join together for the purpose of ordering their own lives in accordance with their religious principles.[3]

The Declaration on Religious Freedom neither denied nor favored separation of church and state. There was clearly a concern also to preserve freedom for parochial schools. Nevertheless, the council did take care to insist on protection of religious freedom where one body should be established by state law. Strong scriptural support was given for the assertion that "in matters religious every manner of coercion on the part of men should be excluded."[4] Such statements doubtless referred to countries like Spain where religious liberty depended on an arrangement with a totalitarian government. Spain has yet to guarantee liberty for any except Roman Catholics. At the same time, the statements reflected the concern of the church that it not be denied freedom, as in Iron Curtain countries.

Conclusion

With this shot in the arm from Roman Catholicism, religious liberty has the strongest support from Christians it has ever had. It has gathered strength in Protestant nations. It is beginning to grow in countries long dominated by the Catholic Church. At the same time absolutely astounding changes have occurred in eastern Europe as first one and then another country has modified its laws to allow free exercise of religion. Nevertheless, there are dangers ahead. Some of the dangers, such as Marxism, stand in full view. Others are hidden. Dangers that are self-evident probably pose a smaller threat to religious liberty's survival than the hidden dangers in free nations like the United States. It is in these nations that vigilance is essential.

For Further Reading

Bradley, Gerhard V. *Church-State Relationships in America.* New York: Greenwood Press, 1987.

Butts, R. Freeman. *The American Tradition on Religion and Education.* Boston: Beacon Press, 1950.

"Declaration on Religious Freedom." *The Documents of Vatican II.* Ed. Walter M. Abbott, S.J. New York: Guild Press, 1966.

Government Intervention in Religious Affairs. Edited by Dean M. Kelley. New York: Pilgrim Press, 1982.

Levy, Leonard W. *The Establishment Clause: Religion and the First Amendment.* New York: Macmillan Co., 1986.

Pfeffer, Leo. *Church, State, and Freedom.* Rev. ed. Boston: Beacon Press, 1967.

For Review

1. Review the discussion of separation of church and state. What is the meaning of "separation of church and state"? How absolute is the "wall of separation"?

2. Why have violations of the constitutional provision of church and state occurred more often at the local or state levels than at the national level?

3. Review areas in which church and state tend to overlap in America to create problems. How have the courts sought to keep a taut line between church and state in these areas?

4. Discuss some of the problem areas in education. What is the source of such problems? What position do you take regarding prescribed prayers, Bible reading, or other religious practices in public schools?

5. Discuss the reasons why the "free exercise of religion" is not unlimited.

6. In what areas does government set boundaries? What principles do the courts usually follow in setting these?

7. Review the growth of religious liberty in Roman Catholicism. When and where did the Roman Catholic Church come out with a clear statement in favor of religious liberty? To what extent did the statement approve separation of church and state?

Notes

1. Leo Pfeffer, *Church, State, and Freedom*, rev. ed. (Boston: Beacon Press, 1967), pp. 661–62.

2. John Courtney Murray, S.J., "Religious Freedom," *The Documents of Vatican II*, ed. Walter M. Abbott, S.J. (New York: Guild Press, 1966), p. 672.

3. Ibid., p. 682.

4. Ibid,, p. 690.

Chapter 9

The Perils of Religious Liberty

RELIGIOUS LIBERTY is a fragile child. If not carefully nurtured and guarded, it may die. Only continuous attention to its health and well-being will assure its survival.

The perils to religious liberty are many. Few, if any, of these are external. Conquest by a foreign power is always one possible way in which freedom may be lost; but in the case of the United States, this seems remote. The more imminent and real dangers are internal. Internal dangers threaten both the nation and religious groups.

National Perils

The most serious danger for religious liberty is to *assume that there is no danger*. It has been a long time since whippings, beatings, imprisonments, and other forms of persecution were handed out to dissenters. "Time heals all wounds," we say. It also causes memory to fade. The tendency is to let down the guard about either separation of church and state or the free exercise of religion.

This danger is heightened by a related one — *assuming that the danger is too slight to bother*. Small incidents seem so unimportant at times that they are glossed over. In education, for example,

131

it is tempting to see such slight danger in small grants for non-religious activities in private or church-related schools that no one bothers to question whether they violate church-state separation. Larger grants are then sought, each time for a slightly broader use. Public funds gradually sustain much of the education program, aspects of which may be indistinguishable from religious education.

The same inattention to small things may threaten the free exercise of religion as well. Many Americans think the Old Order Amish refusal to use safety reflectors on their buggies when they drive over public roads a small and ridiculous item. To the Amish, however, this involves a vital religious principle, prohibition of "worldly" ornamentation. Only an even more significant concern, for personal safety, could justify state enforcement of regulations in violation of Amish religious scruples.

Another danger is posed, especially in times of crisis, by *the sentiment that national safety overrides all freedoms,* including religious ones. In America this sentiment manifested itself during both World Wars in attempted suppression of the speaking of a foreign language in religious services. Thanks to the courts, religious freedom was preserved. However, the danger has not subsided since World War II, for other crises have developed. During the 1950s many persons suffered restriction of religious freedom because of anticommunist fervor.

A rather curious danger to religious liberty arises out of modern psychology and technology. Modern thinkers have devised more effective means to control and shape thought than ancient cultures dreamed possible. Communists have used "brainwashing" techniques with great effectiveness. The Nazis employed similar techniques. Some Westerners, including B. F. Skinner, have advocated the use of psychological techniques to control behavior. The media may be used effectively to shape thought rather than to improve voluntary responses. It is quite possible that such *techniques could be employed to shape religious beliefs and practice in the interest of conformity and subservience to the state.* So far, there have been few signs that this could occur in America, but the danger should not be overlooked.

Christianity's Perils

Christianity has a large stake in the conservation of religious liberty. As a strongly missionary faith, Christianity is concerned not merely to preserve toleration but to preserve also the right to evangelize. Where religious liberty is limited, Christianity's discharging of its mission will be limited. The dangers should be more clearly perceived by Christians than by any other religious group. All too often they are not.

One danger is *inattention to the issue*. Inattention grows readily when religious groups achieve majority status as they have in the United States. Even Baptists, who have done so much to achieve liberty, have let their zeal dwindle. "Unfortunately," James E. Wood, Jr. commented, "many Baptists in the United States today lack any real awareness, knowledge, or understanding of this historic Baptist witness to religious liberty."[1]

Majority status not only has dampened concern, it has tended to create an *establishment mentality*, one that seeks special favors for the majority. A review of history shows that concern for religious liberty is a minority concern. The majority will press for advantages. After Constantine's conversion, Christians who had pleaded for liberty happily received imperial favors. The Puritans who pleaded for freedom in England established themselves in the American colonies. In subtle ways, despite the guarantees of the Constitution, Protestants sometimes have taken advantage of their majority in the United States to assure dominance in public life. Catholics, Jews, and minority religions have struggled to keep the balance.

A more serious danger lurks behind and explains the establishment mentality. This is *the failure to maintain a wholesome balance between concern for the Christian mission and concern for liberty*. It is easy, as much persecution has demonstrated, to let monotheism be narrowed so that God is not seen as the God of all. When this happens, concern to make converts may override concern for liberty.

Such reasoning may take extreme forms. It has been the main source of persecution of Christians by Christians. Persons have been compelled not merely to be Christians but to adopt a certain Christian creed. They have been stretched over a rack on account of theological hairs, such as that "Mary is the Mother of Christ" rather than that "Mary is the Mother of God." It was this danger that prompted Baptists and other dissenters to refuse to give creeds status in their faith and practice.

It is quite possible to say: "We should not require creeds just to be members of a church. However, we must have them for those who hold leading positions in the churches, for the teachers in seminaries, and for denominational leaders." This is the reasoning that initiated persecution of Christians by Christians in the time of Constantine. The first to be imprisoned and sent into exile were leaders. When suppression of their activities did not stop the movements they led, the range of suppression was widened. It eventually included everyone.

A persecutor mentality is fueled by a practical concern, to win converts. The motive for winning converts is heightened by conservatism, particularly a conservatism that approaches bigotry. "We've got something nobody else has got. Outside our group, there is no salvation!" Such thinking fired the early Christian zeal for winning the Roman Empire. Although the concern to win others was commendable in itself, it also fired zeal to the point of violence. No one has shown greater evangelistic zeal than inquisitors and crusaders. They did what they did out of genuine concern to win others. In the light of their goal, the eternal salvation of those they persecuted, even physical tortures did not seem too extreme.

Evangelistic concern may generate a related danger, *seeking ways to evangelize through civil religion*. Evangelical motives have prompted many well-meaning Christians to argue for Bible reading and prescribed prayers in public schools. "America is a Christian nation," they contend. "It must show that to the world." As commendable as the motives may be, such statements reflect the kind of thinking that led Constantine to establish Christianity as the religion of the Roman Empire. Little by little, it led him to suppress other religions and then to suppress different forms of Christianity.

Whether any nation can be called "Christian" is debatable. The conviction that it should be, however, opens a wide door for intolerance. America is today a pluralistic nation, one having many religions. Christians represent a majority. They are not the whole population. In such a situation it is essential that the state manifest no public signs of dominance by any religion. Not even majority status should obtain special recognition for any group. The only hope for conserving religious liberty is to keep the reign of Caesar and the reign of God in their proper spheres.

A Curious Turn

Religious liberty has taken a strange turn in the United States. The religious right professes concern for religious liberty just as vigorously as early Baptists did, but they view it from a very different vantage point, obtaining freedom to effect the kind of society they envision for America. According to their interpretation, the religion of secular humanism has quietly taken control of the country and put a lock on the religious liberty of others. A "this-worldly" religion, an inheritance from ancient Greece, humanism maintains control by keeping the Judaeo-Christian tradition out of public life, especially the schools, where it espouses atheism, evolution, amorality, and collectivism. If Christians want to recover the place their forebears assigned to the Judaeo-Christian tradition, they must wake up to what has happened and fight for the recovery of the liberty the nation's founders intended through voting, legal action, and legislation.

"Freedom," according to Jerry Falwell, a major figure in the new Christian right, "is conditioned upon precisely that — the acknowledgement of and obedience to the laws of our Creator."[2] America's survival depends on the maintenance of its founders' biblical commitments. "It is time for Americans to come back to the faith of our fathers, to the Bible of our fathers, to the biblical principles that our fathers used as a premise for this nation's establishment."[3] The founders did not intend the separation of God from government. American Christians must return the nation to the traditional values taught by the Bible that humanism has eroded. They must restore God to government and God to schools.

Key to getting America back to God is the family, "the fundamental building block and the basic unit of our society," and the unit on which the nation's health depends. Families came to these shores originally "in search of freedom to educate their children according to religious principles."[4] Unfortunately they no longer have such freedom; they are under siege by many evils —

a children's rights movement "neglecting absolutes,"[5] feminism linked to the Equal Rights Amendment, abortion, homosexuality, degraded forms of television, pornography, rock music, drugs and alcohol, and humanistic education.

At one time American schools were the best in the world, that is, when Bible reading and prayer had a prominent role in them. Since the Second World War, however, secular humanism has taken over and forced these out of the curriculum. Public school textbooks have deleted basic values — Judaeo-Christian morality, respect for the nation's heritage, benefits of free enterprise. "Prayer and Bible reading were taken out of the schools because they might 'offend' some child who did not believe in God," Falwell charged. "The other 99 percent of the children had to listen to evolution and secularism, humanism, and vulgarity."[6]

Religious rightists have responded to the perceived threats in several ways. One was to found alternative schools. "Christian schools," Falwell argued, "are the only hopes of training young men and women who will be capable of taking the helm of leadership in every level of society."[7] A powerful boost for such schools came from "white flight" after the U.S. Supreme Court ordered integration of public schools in 1954. The cost of maintaining them, however, put Christian conservatives in a difficult position to compete with better funded public schools. Consequently, with Roman Catholics, many pressed for relief through tax credits for tuition and other means. In addition, Christian schools did not find the freedom they hoped to find in church-sponsored education. In the United States the states have regulated curricula for education for a long time. The required public curricula included items such as evolution and sex education to which conservatives have objected vehemently. In instances where they wanted to receive public assistance, moreover, they put themselves in danger of still closer regulation.

A second conservative response to perils to the society they envision has aimed at changing public education through legislation. Religious rightists have aimed their salvos at the elimination of the Judaeo-Christian heritage from textbooks, the introduction of sex education, the teaching of evolution, and the tilt toward humanism in the whole process. In Texas, Mel and Norma Gabler, a husband and wife team, have worked hard to have textbooks rewritten.

In many states other conservatives have organized effectively to eliminate sex education classes or, where that proved impossible, to force revamping of their content and character. Under conservative pressures several southern state legislatures, Louisiana and Arkansas being the most widely publicized, passed laws subsequently declared unconstitutional that required schools to teach creation science alongside evolution. On a national scale new Christian rightists have pressed for an amendment to the U.S. Constitution opening the way for prayer in public schools. To counter interpretations of the First Amendment by the Supreme Court, they supported an amendment proposed by President Ronald Reagan reading: "Nothing in this Constitution shall be construed to prohibit individual or group prayer in public schools or other public institutions. No person shall be required by the United States or by any state to participate in prayer." In several states Religious rightists sought to secure posting of the Ten Commandments in schools and public buildings and to encourage reading of the Bible in classrooms.

A third conservative response was to gear up for political action. Long quite passive and uninvolved in politics, during the 1970s and 1980s "evangelicals" rallied first behind "born again" Southern Baptist Jimmy Carter and then, with still greater fervor, Ronald Reagan, who promised to help them effect the moral and spiritual revolution they coveted. In pursuit of this objective, Jerry Falwell put together a curious coalition in Moral Majority "to represent our convictions to our government." Moral Majority focused on registration and information with the objective of mobilizing the grass roots. At local, state, and national levels they pressed for legislation to sever humanist control and to assert the Judaeo-Christian vision. Above all, America must return to the Bible.

A fourth conservative response was to undertake a conservative resurgence within the churches. Virtually all denominations in the United States have experienced a push from the religious right. The latter have registered their most remarkable success, however, in the Lutheran Church–Missouri Synod and in the Southern Baptist Convention, the largest Protestant denomination in the United States. Since 1979, fundamentalists have controlled the presidency of the Southern Baptist Convention and, with it, the appointive process through which they can control the institutions supported by this denomination. So successful has been the takeover that, in 1989, Jerry Falwell, though not a Southern Baptist, chose the annual convention in Las Vegas to announce the phasing out of Moral Majority. My personal interpretation of this is that he no longer needed Moral Majority to achieve the goals of the religious right; he now has the Southern Baptist Convention!

The Baptist Tradition: An Endangered Species

Many Baptists will find it strange indeed that the Southern Baptist Convention has become a partner in the religious right coalition, for Baptists in the South played a major role in shaping First Amendment rights. Although some groups of Baptists found a measure of tolerance in Virginia under the Toleration Act of 1689, Separate Baptists, who migrated southward after the Great Awakening and constituted one of the main branches for the Southern Baptist Convention, encountered considerable hostility on account of their evangelistic zeal. Their noisy meetings often triggered mob reaction and then, after 1770, civil action. No group had more to gain from laws favoring complete religious liberty than the Separate Baptists, and they took the most extreme positions on that side. They ardently opposed all confessions of faith, for instance, on the grounds that the Bible alone suffices. Anticreedalism was strongly manifest in the forming of the Southern Baptist convention in 1845 with no doctrinal statement at all for its base. The convention did not adopt any confessional statement until eighty years after it began. How, then, has this remarkable transition occurred?

Basically, the answer to the question is: as a consequence of success. In the southern United States, east of Texas and south of the Mason-Dixon Line, Southern Baptists have become "the Catholic Church of the South." They have grown from a small and despised sect into the dominant denomination. In virtually every county in this area they represent anywhere from 25 to 100 percent of the population. The shift from minority to majority status has resulted in a loss of Baptist consciousness concerning the voluntary principle (soul competency), religious liberty, the separation of church and state, and voluntary cooperation in discharging the world mission of Christ. Recent actions taken by the Southern Baptist Convention clearly confirm the departure from these principles.

Southern Baptists who support the agenda of the religious right still affirm liberty of conscience for individuals. Everyone, they will say, has the right to believe what they want. That freedom, however, does not apply to persons employed within the denomination's agencies. If employed by the latter, then they must think and teach what the denomination decrees. As graphically expressed by Adrian Rogers, then president of the convention, "If we [presumably Southern Baptists] believe pickles have souls and they [professors in the seminaries or other denominational employees] can't teach it, then they shouldn't take our money." Recently the trustees of the Southern Baptist Theological Seminary in Louisville, Kentucky, imposed guidelines for employment, tenuring, and promoting of faculty drawn from the "Findings" of the Peace Committee Report adopted by the Southern Baptist Convention in 1986. The "Findings" consist of specific views of Scripture: that Adam and Eve were real persons, that stated authors of all biblical writings are the actual authors, that miracles reported in the Bible are accurate, and that historical writings of the Bible are accurate in detail.

Resolutions adopted by the Southern Baptist Convention since 1979 reflect clearly an effort to incorporate the perspective of the religious right. At New Orleans in 1982 the convention adopted a resolution favoring the proposed Reagan amendment on prayer in public schools and a second urging that public schools teach "scientific creationism." At Pittsburgh in 1983 the convention, having a more balanced constituency, reiterated traditional Baptist concerns about religious liberty but gave several nods in the direction of the religious right. It encouraged Southern Baptists "to oppose efforts to use governmental institutions and processes to promote the particular interests of a religious constituency" but went on to add "or by favoring those who believe in no religion over those who have a faith commitment."[8] At Kansas City in 1984 the convention adopted a resolution emphatically favoring legislation requiring schools to grant equal access to religious groups. A second resolution, denouncing secular humanism, urged Southern Baptists "to work to reverse the de facto exclusion of references to the Deity from public schools, which makes the gov-

ernment not neutral to religion but antagonistic to it, and replaces
the Judaeo-Christian ethic with a religion of secular humanism."[9] It
also enjoined them "to become personally involved in public, private, or Christian school matters, encouraging the restoration of
theistic principles in the curriculum; ... "[10] In 1986 at Atlanta the
convention spoke again on the First Amendment and religious liberty from the perspective of the religious right. Interpreting the free
exercise clause as "necessarily" including "the liberty to honor God
in word and deed in every legitimate human activity," a resolution
decried Supreme Court "rulings which deny the right of voluntary prayer and Bible reading in the public schools" and urged
Southern Baptists "to become active participants in the political
life of this country — at the local, state, and federal levels — in
order to defend and promote the traditional Judaeo-Christian values necessary if America is to survive as a nation founded upon
those values."[11] Another resolution decried "the virtual total cen-
sorship" in textbooks "of the existence, history, contributions, and
current role of the Judaeo-Christian heritage" and urged prayer,
active opposition, and correction of this.[12] At St. Louis in 1987 the
convention reaffirmed this resolution.

Many of the resolutions noted above indicate that separation of
church and state is no longer axiomatic among Southern Baptists.
At the Pastors' Conference in Dallas in 1985 Presbyterian evange-
list James Kennedy received a standing ovation when he declared
that separation of church and state was not only not a Baptist doctrine but a "heresy." Reminders that "separation of church and
state does not mean separation of God from government" have
become a kind of cliché for the religious right. Richard Land, director of the Christian Life Commission, dismisses fears that the
churches might violate this principle. "Only the government can
violate the First Amendment," he said in a recent address.[13]

Meanwhile the principle of voluntary association has under-
gone considerable reshaping. Strongly influenced by the Church
Growth Movement, many Southern Baptists accentuate pastoral
authority as the key to strong and effective churches. Accordingly, at San Antonio in 1988 the Southern Baptist Convention
minimized the doctrine of the priesthood of the believer as "a recent historical development" in Southern Baptist life and warned
against its use "to justify wrongly the attitude that a Christian may

believe whatever he (or she) chooses and still be considered a loyal Southern Baptist" or "to justify the undermining of pastoral authority in the local church." While affirming acceptance of the doctrine, the convention resolved, among other things, that it "in no way contradicts the biblical understanding of the role, responsibility, and authority of the pastor which is seen in the command to the local church in Hebrews 13:17, 'Obey your leaders, and submit to them; for they keep watch over your souls, as those who will give an account' " and affirmed "the truth that elders, or pastors, are called of God to lead the local church (Acts 20:28)."[14] W. A. Criswell, pastor of the First Baptist Church of Dallas, subsequently declared that lay-led churches will be "weak" churches. An autocratic corporation model in which the pastor has absolute authority has imposed itself on many Southern Baptist congregations, especially large ones.

What lies behind the remarkable shift in Baptist thinking in the American South? Several factors have doubtless played roles. (1) Pluralism: A multiplicity of ideologies constantly compete with one another in the United States. Every religious group faces a challenge to its identity. (2) The mottled character of the churches: Every congregation is mixed, representing a whole array of traditions. Unless leaders make a serious effort to inculcate their heritage and ideal, identity will become confused. (3) Deterioration of church training: Until about 1970 Southern Baptists effectively educated the bulk of their constituency in the Baptist ideal. Since then, however, church training has dropped precipitously with grave consequences, and Southern Baptists have not found the right prescription to cure the ailment. (4) The electronic churches: In the United States the religious right dominates the media. Many Southern Baptists look to Jerry Falwell, Pat Robertson, Charles Stanley, and Adrian Rogers, all of whom have national programs, to discover what being Christian and Baptist means in today's world. If they do not receive solid grounding in Baptist tradition in their local churches, they will equate the principles of the religious right with that tradition. (5) Deliberate efforts to reinterpret the tradition of religious liberty: Some have effectively sought to reconstruct the American story, particularly by equating the intention of the writers of the Constitution with that of the Puritan forebears. According to the reconstructionists, the Puritans came in search of freedom to establish the kind of Christian commonwealth they could not attain in England. The authors of the Declaration of Independence and the U.S. Constitution intended the same thing, as references to God in both would indicate.

Finally (6), success: Since World War II, the Southern Baptist Convention has grown rapidly, overtaking the Methodist Church as the largest single Protestant denomination. The convention's status in the South, where it has its "empire," has subtly eroded its minority perceptions. In Utah, where Mormons dominate, Southern Baptists do not favor prayer in public schools; in Georgia they do; in Utah Mormons would write the prayers, in Georgia Southern Baptists would.

Delicate Balances

The health and survival of religious liberty depend on the maintenance of delicate balances. One is the balance between church and state. Governments should neither be hostile nor show favoritism to religion. They will aid religious groups most by maintaining freedom to engage in their varied activities. If the American experiment has proved anything, it has proved that voluntarism will work.

Another is the balance between complete religious freedom and the limitations required for the good of the society. Liberty of conscience involves an unlimited freedom. God alone has access to human conscience. Liberty to speak, to assemble, and to engage in activities of a religious nature are limited freedoms. In these areas the balance is precarious. Many factors affect it. A state should go as far as possible to favor complete liberty, but the freedom of one person ends where the freedom of another person begins.

For Christians there is another balance. This is the balance between missionary zeal and concern for religious liberty. Missionary zeal must never be so uncontrolled that it allows the end to override the means. I would check this balance by universal monotheism and God's nature as love. God is the God of all humanity and is concerned for the salvation of all. God has not been left without a witness to all. Because of love, God has willed that all persons respond freely. Love never coerces. God never asks those who witness for God to use any means of persuasion stronger than the force of love. In the end, human beings must leave to God alone the judgment of human responses. No human being has the knowledge or the authority to judge. Love is patient. It will wait for God to decide.

For Further Reading

Collier, Stephen T. "Southern Baptists and Selected Church-State Issues: Changing Attitudes and Action, 1960–1976." Unpublished Ph.D. dissertation, Southern Baptist Theological Seminary, Louisville, Ky, 1978.

Morey, Robert A. *The New Atheism and the Erosion of Freedom.* Minneapolis: Bethany House Publishers, 1986.

Noonan, John Thomas. *The Believer and the Powers That Are: Cases, History, and Other Data Bearing on the Relation of Religion and Government.* New York: Macmillan Co., 1982.

For Review

1. List the national perils to religious liberty.

2. List Christianity's perils with regard to soul liberty.

3. List the delicate balances that must be maintained if soul liberty is to be preserved.

Notes

1. "Religious Liberty and Public Affairs in Historical Perspective," *Baptist History and Heritage* (July 1974): 154.

2. *Listen! America* (Garden City, N.Y.: Doubleday & Co., 1980), p. 26.

3. Ibid., p. 43.

4. Ibid., p. 104.

5. Ibid., p. 120.

6. Ibid., p. 182.

7. Ibid., p. 189f.

8. *1980 SBC Proceedings,* p. 63.

9. *1984 SBC Proceedings,* p. 64.

10. Ibid., p. 85.

11. *1986 SBC Proceedings*, p. 75.

12. Ibid., p. 76.

13. Chapel lecture, November 4, 1990, Southern Baptist Theological Seminary.

14. *1988 SBC Proceedings*, p. 69.